LEADING
WELL

culture in which Black Christian women have a predestined place and purpose. This book summons us to class . . . at the well."

Dr. Carolyn D. Showell, author of *Discovering Wisdom in Chaos* and president and founder of the Women's Institute of Learning and Leadership

"As an African American, Christian, woman entrepreneur, I needed *Leading Well* when my career and life journey began decades ago. It points with precision to the issues, difficulties, challenges, joys, privileges, and realities of being a Black woman in America. I have heard many sermons and lessons about the Samaritan woman at the well with Jesus. None have illuminated the poignant lessons of this well-known biblical story so profoundly. You will surely see yourself in the pages of this inspirational and empowering book. Jeanne shares transparently and lavishly from her own experiences in a way that makes her supremely relatable and relevant. While reading *Leading Well*, you will feel like Jeanne is a girlfriend, mentor, instructor, coach, and sister all at once. *Leading Well* helps the reader ask important questions of herself that are necessary for self-discovery, growth, and liberation. This book is a deep well of insight, instruction, encouragement, and wisdom. *Leading Well* is a must-read for Black women and our allies. It will move readers to a place of greater fulfillment and effectiveness."

Dr. Debbye Turner Bell, CEO/founder of Debbye Turner Bell Consulting, author of *Courageous Faith*, pastor, veterinarian, and Miss America 1990

"If you're leading at a feverish pitch, exhausted, short on patience and peace, and thin on time with Jesus, this is YOUR book. Practical, wise, and spiritually vibrant, *Leading Well* offers barrier-breaking, soul-centered strategies for women in racist, sexist cultures."

Mimi Haddad, PhD, president of CBE International

"We are living in a time that desperately needs insightful, spiritual, and truthful leadership! In *Leading Well*, Jeanne shares her decades of professional experience, wealth of knowledge, and biblical insight to empower Black women leaders to live into their authentic identity and reach their full, God-given potential. If you're a leader who is ready to reimagine leadership with principles and practices that will bring new life and longevity to your work and ministry, this book is for you!"

Dr. Brenda Salter McNeil, author of *Becoming Brave* and *Roadmap to Reconciliation*

"Jeanne offers us a long-awaited and desperately needed spiritual road map for Black women's leadership. Attentive to the unique challenges and cultivated strengths of such leaders, Jeanne provides an insightful narrative, rich biblical exposition and application, and practical steps. In this book, we are seen, valued, equipped, and exhorted to faithful leadership."

Christina H. Edmondson, PhD, Certified Cultural Intelligence facilitator, public speaker, mental health therapist, and coauthor of *Faithful Antiracism*

"I always pay close attention to the writings of Jeanne Porter King. It is because I know her to be a critical and progressive thinker who passionately advocates for 'Justice' in both secular and sacred societies. Once again, through the narrative of another woman's story, Jeanne creates a pedagogy designed to teach us how to reclaim, reimagine, and reframe our experience of 'being and becoming' Black Christian women who lead. This book invites us to see through new lenses as we step into the Gospel of John chapter 4. We are enlightened by principles and practices by which we can live 'in' and live 'out' King's fresh revelations needed in these uncertain times. We are empowered to push through the restricting barriers into the dimension of spirituality, which fuels all other dimensions of our existence.

"This book is an inspired model written for our healing, health, and wellbeing.

"I highly recommend this book to everyone whose assignment is to heal the world and establish the kingdom counterculture in the earth. A

LEADING WELL

A BLACK WOMAN'S GUIDE TO WHOLISTIC,
BARRIER-BREAKING LEADERSHIP

JEANNE PORTER KING

BakerBooks

a division of Baker Publishing Group
Grand Rapids, Michigan

Published by Baker Books
a division of Baker Publishing Group
Grand Rapids, Michigan
www.bakerbooks.com

Printed in the United States of America

Library of Congress Cataloging-in-Publication Data
Names: King, Jeanne Porter, 1959– author.
Title: Leading well : a Black woman's guide to wholistic, barrier-breaking leadership / Jeanne Porter King.
Description: Grand Rapids, Michigan : Baker Books, a division of Baker Publishing Group, 2023. | Includes bibliographical references.
Identifiers: LCCN 2022051807 | ISBN 9781540902962 (paperback) | ISBN 9781540903235 (casebound) | ISBN 9781493441198 (ebook)
Subjects: LCSH: Leadership in minority women. | Christian leadership. | Women, Black.
Classification: LCC HQ1163 .K564 2023 | DDC 303.3/40820973—dc23/eng /20230309
LC record available at https://lccn.loc.gov/2022051807

Some names and details have been changed to protect the privacy of the individuals involved.

The author is represented by the literary agency of Embolden Media Group, LLC.

Baker Publishing Group publications use paper produced from sustainable forestry practices and post-consumer waste whenever possible.

23   24   25   26   27   28   29   7   6   5   4   3   2   1

I dedicate this book to my mother, Marjorie Stella Porter.
Mom, you taught me to love well.
My heart overflows with gratitude for you.

CONTENTS

INTRODUCTION

Chances are, as a Black woman leader, you have been asked at some point to define leadership—what it is, how it looks from your vantage point, and how to achieve a similar paid or volunteer role. Over the years, I've answered those same queries many times. Because answers vary, let's start with a foundational definition. For purposes of this book, *leading* is the process of influencing, making an impact, and providing guidance and wisdom, whether we have a title or not.

As Black women of faith, leading also includes being the light and a representative of Christ wherever we have been called.

Like our hair textures, colors, lengths, and styles, Black Christian women's leadership is diverse. Leadership looks different on each of us! Yet when it comes to execution of our roles, one similarity is worth pursuit. We can—and should—lead *well*. What does that mean?

Leading well is foremost leading effectively. Effective leaders fulfill their assignments and execute responsibilities with excellence and maximum impact. I believe leading well also means leading from a place of wholeness, whereby Black Christian women are empowered by the Spirit of God for maximum output with minimal negative impact on ourselves and others. Thus, for purposes of this book, I define leading well as a wholistic[1] approach based on leading from the inside out—from the wellspring of living water that Jesus promised. It is the type of leadership that equips, empowers, rejuvenates, and inspires us to serve in the church and the marketplace as a calling.

Black women lead. And more of us want to lead in a way that does not cause detriment to our souls. Basically, we want to lead well. What does that look like from a Black woman's perspective? The answer is quite simple but becomes complicated when adopting a majority-culture definition of leadership and *then* placing an unreasonable performance burden on the backs and shoulders of Black women leaders. That is akin to defining our hair by majority-culture standards of beauty—a self-defeating task! The simple truth, however, is that just as our hair is naturally beautiful and created by God to display God's glory, leading well for Black women is both natural and God-centered.

Black women lead in every area of society. Some of us reading this book are corporate executives or managers seeking to rewire our leadership. Some are considering entering new leadership roles. Some lead in churches and community agencies. Some lead as volunteers in service organizations. Still others are retired, now helping to raise grandchildren.

This book is for all of us.

I offer this book as a resource for us to cope with the exclusion we experience in the workplace but also to empower us to wholistically lead from the well of the Spirit.

Unfortunately, many of us are pushed to the margins—or beyond—while leading. As Black women, many of us lead within our organizations and institutions as outsiders, not fully embraced or included. That outsider status gives us a distinct perspective. As Black women, we experience the dual assaults of racism and sexism, which come in both blatant ways and in subtler forms of comments or actions in our workplaces and communities that hurt our hearts. These take their toll on our lives. It's time for a change.

Sometimes the organizational cultures in which we lead are not inclusive and don't respect, embrace, or get the diverse perspectives we bring to the table. So many of us are encouraged to fit into a leadership mold that doesn't always fit so well. These old leadership models are like shoes that are too tight—restrictive and limiting our freedom and mobility.

Still, other Black women leaders hold back a little of our authentic identity to be perceived as fitting into the culture at work or church. Some of us stay in places in which we have been and continue to be excluded no matter how hard we work and no matter our achievements.

. . . . .

Because of other people's perspectives, we have not always felt we could bring our whole selves to our leadership contexts. And many of us surely don't believe we can care for ourselves before we care for everyone else. These stressors leave their mark on our souls, and those marks affect our ability to lead well.

This is what happened in Angel's case.

A midlevel leader in a financial services company, Angel had received numerous accolades while leading her team and projects with exemplary results. Yet, as the only Black woman on a team of fifty, she felt she had to prove herself every day despite her accomplishments. Angel also had to dodge the daily subtle and not so subtle racist and sexist darts thrown at her by her manager and some of her colleagues.

The pressurized environment wore Angel out! Angel led effectively, but she wasn't leading well. She wrote me, letting me know she was physically, mentally, and spiritually drained and needed guidance from a Christian woman who has led in business.

Then there was Tameka. Like Angel, Tameka also dealt with on-the-job comments designed to undermine her leadership. Outwardly she was successful, but inwardly she felt as if she was drowning. Hardworking and confident, she successfully met her work-related goals. Yet internally she was tired with a capital *T*.

She struggled with how to show up in meetings. That was not always the case, but sharing a viewpoint different from those of some coworkers had put Tameka on her manager's radar. Her manager pulled her aside and told her she needed to be a better team player.

Grappling with toeing the line or sharing her perspective, Tameka was stumped. Should she speak up or not? She feared if she didn't say anything in those meetings, her coworkers would assume she was not adding value, and they'd overlook her input and ability to succeed. Her confidence was waning, and Tameka had lost the joy in a job she once loved.

Perhaps you can relate to Angel's or Tameka's leadership trials— or maybe your situation is more like Jessica's. She had discovered that proven leadership skills welcomed in one place may not be embraced in another. Specifically, she had demonstrated a lot of leadership ability in her church and community and was looking to live out a more purpose-filled life at work.

Jessica worked in human resources. She wanted to move into a leadership role that enabled her to use *all* of her gifts, talents, and experiences. But she couldn't catch a break on her 9-to-5, despite her leadership acumen outside the walls of her company. Sadly, she felt so excluded from advancement opportunities that she was considering a job or career change.

· · · · ·

These examples reveal how Black Christian women leaders face myriad limitations in our leadership, development, and advancement. Lived experiences of women like Angel, Tameka, and Jessica also underscore the great need for a book like *Leading Well*. Too often, we lead in places where the leaders we work for or with define success in merely quantitative terms. A higher return on investment, productivity, engagement scores, sales, and number of speaking engagements are the measures of leadership success. Still others define success by the title on the nameplate of their door or other accruals such as fancy cars, houses, and planes.

But do those things count in and of themselves in the grand scheme of things? Instead, isn't our challenge as women of faith to create meaning and purpose? Isn't that why we spend so much time carving out the correct mission statement to connect people in our organizations to broader purposes? Isn't that why, after two years of a global pandemic, the world has experienced an exodus from workplaces of people seeking meaning and purpose?

In 2022, 70 percent of "C-suite level executives seriously considered resigning for a job that better support[ed] their wellbeing."[2] In addition, 86 percent of executives "said the pandemic ha[d] negatively affected their overall health," and 81 percent "said improving their own equilibrium [was] more important than advancing their careers right now."[3] I believe these "exiters" aspire to lead well and not sacrifice their health and wellbeing at the altar of corporate and institutional systems.

For Black women of faith who lead, the priority of our wellbeing must become baked into our leadership systems. No longer can we afford to coach and train leaders, especially women leaders, on caring for the organization without caring for ourselves. We must develop the whole leader. Leadership skills and organizational goals cannot take precedence over our wellbeing. I offer this message of leading in this book so that we can advance the human flourishing of all of us.

My Early Leadership Journey

For me, leadership is ultimately a spiritual journey. Regardless of the number of courses we take or how many leadership competencies we develop, ultimately, our effectiveness will hinge on the state of our souls. *Literally!*

That's because, as Christians, we lead from who we are in the depths of our souls, and what we do emanates from our innermost being. At least we are supposed to do so. But too many of us get caught in the tsunami of leadership models that prioritize performance over people. For believers, truly leading well means leading from a place of internal wholeness. It means leading from the "well" within us and resisting the external cacophony of voices pressuring, cajoling, and calling for assimilation to the world's models.

As believers, and specifically believing Black women, leading from our spiritual core sustains us even in the most trying situations. In my early days of working as a corporate consultant while simultaneously serving in ministry in my local church, I fell into a performance trap. I traveled extensively, working with leaders across the country. I developed training sessions that taught skills or developed processes that enhanced the effectiveness of teams and organizations.

While I was doing all this traveling, I was also serving in church and ministry leadership. And like many of us do, I fell into the routine of performing according to external standards and benchmarks without calculating the hidden toll my drive was exacting upon my soul. I counted my success based on the number of new clients I brought in and maintained, the number of engagements I agreed to per year, the number of new affiliate team members I added, and, of course, the amount of revenue I brought in. These external measures were important, but they couldn't sustain me.

Inside I kept sensing a need to change how I led and developed leaders. I needed to shift from leading to fulfill only external measures to leading from the inside out—that is, from a place of purpose, values, and wholeness.

I had to transform from leading like a "superwoman" to becoming—and leading as—a "well woman."

Leading like a superwoman entails acting as if we have the capacity to do all things for all people—all by ourselves! It's the mindset that we can keep piling more and more responsibilities and tasks on our plates and somehow get forty-eight hours of work done in a twenty-four-hour day—every day. An impossible goal, but a superwoman mentality nevertheless compels working ourselves to the bone without giving our spirits, souls, and bodies the rest they deserve through daily lunch breaks, weekly Sabbath observation, yearly vacations, and the like.

Acting like a superwoman is never advantageous and often stems from brokenness. When we lead like this we don our cape and handle our business without missing a beat. We don't delegate or count on others to get the job done. We push ourselves to the point of exhaustion. And we don't slow down long enough to reflect, rest, and get revived.

I know some sister leaders proudly proclaim their superwoman status. Been there, done that. For me, that path did not lead to superhuman strength, insight, or power but to a breakdown.

Leading from that broken place—being overstressed and overstretched—was good neither for the people I served nor myself. Since then I've learned how to integrate wellness principles and practices into my approach to leadership so I could start from a healthier place and cultivate healthier practices for the people and places I serve.

The lessons I share with you in *Leading Well* emerge from my journey of learning to do just that. My journey started many years ago, and at different junctures the Spirit has prodded me to reexamine my leadership practices. I didn't realize it at the time, but at each new stage in my life, the Holy Spirit put me on a path toward what I now call leading well.

Perhaps you're sensing the Spirit nudging you to reexamine your leadership practices. Or perhaps external forces, including the COVID-19 pandemic, have caused you to seek a more sustainable and wholistic leadership model. If so, *Leading Well* is for you.

Black Women and Wellness

Leading Well is based on a wellness framework that focuses on the spiritual dimension of our lives. According to the Global Wellness

Institute, "wellness is multidimensional," and most wellness models "include at least six dimensions."[4] These dimensions might include mental, spiritual, emotional, social, environmental, and physical wellness. Some models add lifestyle while others add a financial dimension, and still others add an occupational category. The intent is to acknowledge that each dimension of our lives is interrelated, and each area affects our overall wellbeing.

Uniquely, this book focuses on spirituality but not as one equal dimension of six, nine, or twelve factors. Instead, *Leading Well* focuses on spiritual wellness for Black women as the core of our wellbeing so that we might truly lead well. We will learn that the spiritual wellness we yearn for comes from the overflowing well of the Spirit Jesus promised in John 4:14.

It is worth noting that the wellness models I've found don't include a couple of dimensions I know to be vital to our wellbeing as Black women. For instance, none address a healthy identity as a critical dimension of wellness or wellbeing. *Leading Well* bridges that information gap, centering Black women's identity as a critical component to effective leadership. Why is this important?

So often, Black women carry what Dr. Chanequa Walker-Barnes calls the burden of strength.[5] As I noted above, the Black Superwoman (or Strong Black Woman) image creates a type of leadership in which we try to be everything to everyone with no reserves left for ourselves. I'll say more about that later. For now, know that embracing our God-given identity is essential, especially in a world that doesn't fully affirm Black women.

Finally, leading for Black women is ingrained in our culture. Black female excellence is a cultural value. Ask Mary McLeod Bethune. Lifting as we climb is a cultural value. Ask Mary Church Terrell. Leading liberation is a cultural value. Ask Harriet Tubman. Leading for justice for our communities is a cultural value. Ask Ida B. Wells. The culture, tradition, and legacy of Black women who came before us serve as inspiration for leading well, whether we have a title or not.

Our cultural heritage, hailing back to an ancient West African worldview, preserves the sense of wellbeing that anchors a leading well mindset and practices for Black women. Our ancestors believed ardently in the spiritual world. In this worldview, there is a sense of wholeness in the entire created order of which we are a part. "A sense of wholeness of the person is manifested in the African attitude to life. Just as there is no separation between the sacred and the secular in communal life, neither is there a separation between the soul and the body in a person."[6]

Our ancestors also believed in the value of our collective humanity. For instance, the South African concept of *ubuntu*, which means "I am because you are," underscores the sense of communal and collective value necessary for our overall wellbeing. Our ancestors held a belief about God and community that our faith tradition celebrates and from which we can draw.

As Black Christian women who lead, we need resources that honor our faith yet equip us to lead effectively in our workplaces, churches, community organizations, and homes. The practices Black women leaders of faith use to draw from the well include prayer, Bible reading, and personal and corporate worship. Let's affirm these. They help us to cope with the exclusion we experience. Both the private and robust communal dimensions to our wellbeing are deeply spiritual. Ultimately, that is what leading well is about.

About This Book

I never thought I'd become an advocate for wellness for Black women leaders. *Leading Well* was conceived after two of my closest friends died a month apart, each from rare cancers, at relatively young ages. These friends were Black women leaders of faith at the top of their game. Competent and charismatic, my friends led with clarity, conviction, and care for their institutions and the people they served. I couldn't shake the thought that their deaths were a wake-up call for me. I searched Scripture for answers.

My friends had accomplished so much in their respective fields, leaving a legacy for the next generation. Their dying reminded me that none of us knows how much time we have on this earth. Their full but relatively short lives epitomized for me the need for each of us to lead well.

We each have moments or seasons that call us to examine our lives and leadership. I've had many such seasons at various junctures of my life. In each, the Spirit beckoned me to draw from the well of living water, and I broke through to a healthier leadership.

You can too.

I'm here to tell you that leading well at work and home is possible. We can earnestly seek self-care resources while caring for our companies, projects, and other people.

I'm also here to tell you that as you strive to lead well, you will encounter challenges. Life happens, and it often happens when we decide to completely follow God in any area, such as in our leadership execution. You *will* be challenged as you read *Leading Well* and work to incorporate its practices and principles. But do not quit.

Please understand that leading well is a journey. It entails making an ongoing commitment to ourselves. The truth is God's love and redemption for humankind are all-embracing and are shared equally with women and men, Black, white, and Brown. God's calling into ministry and leadership—including marketplace leadership—is also given equally to men and women of all cultural backgrounds, including ours.

I offer this book as a resource for Black women leaders. I write to encourage us to use our voices and engage in changing these places for the good of all. I invite Black women of faith to lead from the well within. I also welcome other leaders, especially those who consider themselves our allies, to read this book, as its message is pertinent to all leaders. Still, this book centers Black women and our experiences as Black Christian women.

. . . . .

I have written this book based on the lessons I gleaned from another outsider woman, the Samaritan woman at the well. Remember her?

We find her story in John 4. She was an outsider to the culture of Jesus's day, and she left a legacy of leading that can inform and inspire us all. As a woman from an outsider culture included in the mission of Jesus, her encounter with Jesus provides vital lessons for us today. We've descended upon workplaces and places of worship in great numbers and ascended to the highest ranks of leadership in business, academia, and some religious spheres. And in politics—as Vice President Kamala Harris can attest.

Yet despite our accomplishments, serious patterns of exclusion *still* persist. Patriarchy in every sphere of influence has created a narrative about women's leadership that positions women, especially Black women, as outsiders. Patriarchy is the system of thought and practice that espouses the power of men over women and limits the power of women to lead.

Moreover, books on women's leadership are too often written to give women advice on adapting to a male-dominant system with patriarchal leadership models. For Black women, that advice involves adapting to a system that privileges whiteness *and* maleness. This approach creates an implied narrative about Black women's leadership that positions it as inferior. It encourages us to assimilate to a supposedly superior men's leadership model. Further, it ignores the systems that constrain Black women in leadership.

What is needed is an approach to leadership that challenges and changes that narrative while simultaneously giving Black women tools to strengthen leadership in line with our whole selves. I offer it between these pages.

Here, we will do a reread of the Samaritan woman's story. Too often, she has been the subject of narrative bias, as preachers and teachers have cast her as a "sinful" woman without a redemptive story line. But many who teach or preach about her ignore the cultural context in which she lived. They also minimize what she brought to the dialogue with Jesus. A closer read of the story through the lens of her culture yields more insight into their conversation and how it ignited her leadership.

Her story speaks to us Black women who have likewise been subject to cultural bias and systemic racism and misogyny. Her story reminds us that our relationship with the Lord is the starting place for wholistic leadership in any context for Black women of faith.

Using the Samaritan woman's conversation with Jesus as a guide, I discuss wholistic leadership and offer a series of spiritual lessons on leadership. These aim to reshape the patriarchal narrative about Black women to acknowledge, affirm, and accentuate our resilience and deep reservoirs of strength. These lessons also incorporate what I consider a crucial principle of leading well. Black women leaders must lead from the inside out—that is, from the spiritual well that is within us. These lessons are relevant whether we lead in the marketplace or church. They flow from the living water that replenishes our well—daily.

It is time to honor leadership approaches that stem from our faith and cultural traditions and lead wholistically, creatively, justly, and effectively.

It is time for us to share *our* leadership stories of stepping into our God-given leadership roles.

Our Leading Well Guide

Each chapter of this book will cover one aspect of why and how we can start leading with a wholistic vision of wellness and leadership in mind. In chapter 1, we get started by taking an honest look at the state of our leadership and reimagining what our leadership can be. Chapter 2 covers what it means to be Black women who lead and encourages us to shed stereotypes to lean into the God-given strengths of our multifaceted identities.

Chapter 3 showcases strategies for accessing the wellspring from which healthy leadership flows. Bias can block the flow of our leadership, so in chapter 4 I lay out a strategy for defying this bias. Next, in chapter 5 we delve into how worship helps us perceive more possibilities for our leadership, families, communities, and nations. Chapter 6 will help us own the transformative power that stems from knowing about the dynamics of racism. Chapter 7 focuses on how to prioritize our wellbeing and how to relinquish old mindsets and limiting beliefs.

In chapter 8, I help us reframe our leadership from career to vocation. Chapter 9 offers tools for gaining leadership clarity. Then in chapter 10 we'll discuss the legacy-building power of shared stories. Finally, the appendix offers a road map for developing an ongoing leading well plan.

At the end of each chapter, I provide leading well reflection questions to help us internalize the lessons of that chapter and a leading well practice from one of nine dimensions of wellbeing I have found crucial for Black women. Each practice aims to help us incorporate a wellness discipline into our leadership.

Leading Well Together

So much of what we do as Black women is in community. Please read this book with a friend or a group of sister leaders. Consider recommending it to your book club to read it together. Ask the women's ministry of your church or your sorority chapter to include it in their programming.

Now is the time for integrating wellness principles and practices into our leadership. It begins with learning to lead from the well.

I ask you to stop and consider this question: *What would your life look like if you indeed led from the well?*

Join me in gleaning from the transformative dialogue between this unnamed woman who met Jesus at a well and gleaning from her leadership after the biblical story ends.

ONE

REIMAGINE YOUR LEADERSHIP

[Jesus] had to go through Samaria on the way.

John 4:4

Picture this: you are a midlevel manager months away from your fifteen-year work anniversary. With rapid consolidation in the industry, your position has changed dramatically over the past five years. Due to a recent staff reduction impacting the team you lead, you are working harder and longer and are experiencing more burnout. You feel less motivated about leading in this changing industry. Your mantra has become, "I can't do *this* anymore!" You dream of making a change—using your leadership gifts in more purposeful ways somewhere else. But how?

Change rarely happens in a vacuum or by happenstance. Often circumstances compel leaders to reevaluate priorities or commitments and make deliberate strategic decisions for the future. At

25

times there is an unexpected urgency—a move *now* factor—making it imperative that leaders embrace immediate change!

Because of the pandemic-related shutdown of 2020, I had to make such a change in my business that it led to transforming how I developed and coached leaders. Corporations, government agencies, schools, and other entities sent employees home, established widespread work-from-home procedures, and canceled in-person learning sessions—*literally* two weeks before my scheduled trip to facilitate a women's leadership training program. Thankfully, my client did not cancel their program. Instead, my team and I had five days to pivot to an all-virtual platform.

Pivot.

In leadership circles, *pivot* became the buzzword for the ability to think, act, and execute quickly during the pandemic. Still a rallying cry today, it encompasses flexibility, creativity, and adaptability and is especially important when seeking to maximize new opportunities presented by trying circumstances.

When the client gave the final approval to proceed with the program, she affirmed the true importance of our work. "The class itself can indeed be a welcome diversion and an element of 'self-care' during these unusual times," she said. By highlighting self-care as a reason for continuing with the program, she underscored an essential component of effective leadership. We *cannot* lead well if we don't take care of ourselves—on all fronts.

Typically, self-care isn't one of the stated purposes for leadership development programs, but clearly, March 2020 was not a typical month—and neither were the months and years that followed. Having my client see self-care as a necessary purpose for this program provided me with an early indication of what women leaders, especially Black women leaders, would need moving forward.

In this reimagined space, we permitted ourselves to talk about the stress that came with the uncertainty of the pandemic. That session started a trend I continued to hear about with many other clients throughout the year, as leaders described needing strategies for tending to both their wellbeing and that of their employees.

The pandemic amplified the need to create safe spaces for being authentic and prioritizing our own needs first so we could lead well in our workplaces, homes, and communities. You *know* that need continues!

To be effective leaders, especially as Black women of faith, it is important to reimagine our roles and the possibilities we can have in our leadership if we begin from a place of wholeness. Not from brokenness but from stability. Not from busyness but from purpose. Not from reactiveness but from responsiveness, with an internal sense of clarity and peace.

As leaders, we long to be successful. Often we seek specific outcomes centering on money (*Get that bag, girl!*), position and authority (*Boss lady making boss moves!*), or placement (*Get that corner office, Sistah!*).

Those external factors are important. However, they are rarely foundational elements of leadership models that center wellness, especially for Black women. Rarely do we think about what we need to maintain a healthy spirit, soul, or body—unless something has gone down that stresses us to the breaking point (like the pandemic). Life, then, compels us to reimagine our leadership, develop creative approaches to strategy implementation, and shift to new ways of team building.

A Path Less Traveled

I've mentioned that for me leadership is a spiritual journey. For purposes of *Leading Well*, we will look at the journey Jesus took to a well in Samaria, its impact on the woman of Samaria, and its relevancy for Black Christian women leaders today.

To really appreciate the context for the story we'll be exploring throughout this book, we must start with Jesus coming to Samaria. Yes, our leadership today and the ability to lead well also begin with Jesus. Whether we lead in the marketplace, school, or church, our leadership starts with the Lord's purpose for each of us. Our "why" for leading is critical. Knowing, owning, and expressing that for our leadership is vital to everything we do. Never check your faith at the door. It's what sets us apart—and sets us up to be used by God as transformative leaders.

Tradition in Jesus's day held that instead of traveling through the region of Samaria, Jewish people opted to take a less direct route because of the long-held tensions between the two people groups and their shared history. Yet we see in the story that Jesus *had* "to go through Samaria on the way" to Galilee (John 4:4). His mission compelled Jesus to proclaim the gospel of his kingdom to the Samaritans, so Jesus defied cultural mores and norms to go through Samaria.

There are times when it will be necessary for each of us to go through our own Samaria. It may mean following a path that is new and unpaved. Our God-given mission to lead will compel us to change.

I first experienced this very early in my career, when I was working as an organizational effectiveness consultant on the staff of a Fortune 100 company. After almost five years of work that I loved and was, frankly, good at, I sensed there was much more for me than the corporate grind I was experiencing. The nonstop travel to the various locations across the country that I had initially found exciting began to wear on me.

So I mustered the courage to quit my corporate job and enter graduate school. I was thirty years old and commanding an impressive salary at the time, and some of my close friends and family questioned my choice to leave. "You're leaving that good job?" they chided. They saw the fat salary as a reason to stay, but I considered my wellbeing of much greater value to *me*. No job is worth the cost of our soul's wellbeing.

Know this: as we embark upon a wholistic approach to leadership, we will experience pushback. Everyone won't understand our choices to prioritize our wellbeing, but we've got to be able to listen to the voice within and courageously act accordingly. In the classic *Let Your Life Speak*, spiritual writer Parker Palmer calls it the "voice of vocation."[1] (I'll share more about this in chapter 8.)

Of course, heeding that internal voice may not include leaving a job—but it might! Along the way to heeding my leadership call, I discovered that leadership development is rarely a linear path. When we venture out on God's chosen path for us, it usually includes some twists and turns, and it often requires leaving some places. Following God will mean not allowing naysayers to drown out our internal yea-sayer. It means courageously embracing our distinct paths.

My next step came with accepting and affirming the distinct strengths that I brought to the leadership development field. I was a minister who operated in the marketplace—in corporate, education, and government spaces. I was a Black woman whose perspective and experiences enabled me to offer an underrepresented point of view that added unique insights to leadership conversations in these sectors.

Signs You Need a Change

There will be distinct seasons in our lives when we sense the Lord leading us to make moves that strengthen our leadership in more wholistic ways. We hear this leading as we intentionally carve out time to seek the Lord about our leadership and life.

There are other times in which, because of the pace at which we work or serve, we've become too busy to really hear God. Yet our souls feel the need for change.

When we look at the context of Jesus's going to Samaria, we see conditions that led Jesus to move on. Likewise, these conditions arise around us.

Comparison

Interestingly, the Pharisees noted Jesus made and baptized more disciples than John the Baptist, which led Jesus to journey through Samaria to get to Galilee (John 4:1). Surely Jesus and John did not consider themselves as rivals—or competitors. They each knew their distinct roles and led well in them. Acknowledging they were not in competition, John affirmed that he was sent to spotlight the ministry of Jesus. John even declared his role must decrease, even as Jesus's must increase (3:30). Still the Pharisees, as the keepers of the traditional religious structure, made the comparison.

We should not be surprised!

The structures and systems in which we lead often heighten the tendency toward unhealthy comparison. We are quite satisfied with our work role until we hear about a friend or colleague's promotion and wonder why we didn't get our own promotion. Then we set out to get one too. Unhealthy comparison breeds unhealthy competition.

People who prompt us toward such comparison aren't really interested in us, our callings, or our purposes. They want to know about the size of our staff, the size of our ministries, how much revenue we bring in, or the size of the budgets for which we are responsible. They are trying to quantify our worth in terms of how much more we have than others. But no amount of money or other metrics can appraise our souls! Who we are in Christ anchors our worth: we are children of God, blessed, adopted, chosen, and "accepted in the Beloved" (Eph. 1:6 NKJV)!

Jesus left without setting the record straight. Laser-focused on fulfilling his leadership assignment to go through Samaria, Jesus did not bother addressing the Pharisees' comparison chatter. We later learn through the Gospels that Jesus always led, ministered, and served by following the will of his heavenly Father. He was not in competition with any other leader. Neither was John the Baptist, who readily acknowledged his call as a forerunner of Christ. And neither are we.

Sister leaders, don't miss this. You do not need to compare yourself to anyone else. *Ever.* And you need not fall into comparison traps other people set to lift you up—or tear you down.

As Black women of faith, if we are not careful, we will buy into patriarchal, hierarchal leadership models detrimental to ourselves, the people we serve, and the communities we are trying to build and sustain. That competitive spirit starts with comparison, and according to researcher and bestselling author Brené Brown, comparison "can affect our self-concept, our level of aspiration, and our feelings of well-being."[2] It manifests in jealousy toward others, especially other Black women. We are not in competition with anyone else in terms of our roles, leadership, dress size, hairstyle, bank account, house, apartment, or car we drive. We are not even in competition with ourselves. To establish a healthy foundation for growth, we need to be able to celebrate both our successes and the successes of those around us so we can be the best version of ourselves each day.

When we find ourselves in places where our sense of self is being diminished due to this tendency toward unhealthy comparison, then for our souls' sake, it's time to pivot and reimagine how and where we can lead from our best self and not in competition with others.

Blind Spots

As the gatekeepers of their religion's tradition, the Pharisees protected their authority throughout the Gospels. Understandably, leaders play a crucial role in passing on the culture's values and safeguarding the norms. Yet we must be careful that, as God begins to shift and introduce new perspectives, we can discern that shift and adjust. When Jesus, the new rabbi in town, so to speak, challenged the Pharisees, they bristled against his proclamations of what God was doing. Sister leaders, we don't want to miss what God is purposing to do in our lives because we are stuck in a pattern or way of doing things that is no longer contributing to our wholeness.

Sometimes it's easier to protect the status quo, the way things currently are and have been, than change. Sometimes changing a role feels like an attack on our identity. Our roles as leaders give us such great rewards that who we are can get confused with what we do. But we are more than our roles. If our position changes, our identity does not disintegrate. If the status quo keeps us stuck, it's time to reimagine the way we do things.

When we don't examine our biases, these blind spots can cause us to miss opportunities. We miss them because we don't see them. Jesus defied the accepted, normative biases of his day. He didn't let cultural barriers keep him from his mission, nor did gender barriers or potential class differences stop him from conversing with a Samaritan woman.

If we were raised in a part of our culture that didn't celebrate women as leaders or with people who didn't affirm our voices and what we have to say, we might have blind spots about our own potential. And if we are in a space where those who are in charge have blind spots that make them ignore or undervalue the contributions of women like us, we may have to go where we will be valued. We will need to do the internal work that helps us grow in self-awareness of our worth, skills, and abilities and do the external work of finding places that affirm our gifts and experiences.

Reimagining our leadership will mean getting out of our comfort zones and entering a challenging zone that expands our thinking about our lives and our leadership.

Extreme Busyness

In the story's opening scene, Jesus was sitting at the well in Sychar by himself. "He was alone at the time because his disciples had gone into the village to buy some food" (John 4:8). We don't know how many of his disciples were traveling with him, but I wonder why *all* the disciples who were with him had to go. Couldn't any of them stay behind and just sit with Jesus?

We see this preponderance of activity with his followers throughout the Gospels. Peter wanted to build tabernacles on the Mount of Transfiguration instead of just reveling in the moment of such spectacular glory (Matt. 17:1–8). Martha was so busy working she missed a chance to learn at Jesus's feet, a rare opportunity for women at this time (Luke 10:38–42). James and John were so caught up in strategizing their next promotion, they got their mother to advocate on their behalf and lost sight of what it truly means to lead—serving and sacrificing (Matt. 20:20–23). Jesus's ministry demands were often so great, with "so many people coming and going that Jesus and his apostles didn't even have time to eat" (Mark 6:31). Instead of keeping that pace, Jesus led the apostles to get away and rest.

Leadership demands can be incredibly draining. I understand that. Requests, projects, and programs seem to be nonstop. And when we act like the superwomen we often think we need to be, we'll try to juggle these demands without missing a beat.

Busyness is such a part of leadership culture that leaders brag about it. When I worked in a professional services firm, there seemed to be a competition to see who was the busiest. A conversation with a colleague would go something like this:

"I worked until eight last night getting the proposal together."

"Oh, that's nothing; I left around five, got home and got the kids fed, and then stayed up until midnight finishing my presentation."

Those leaders wanted to earn bragging rights for who could be the busiest and seemingly most productive. But doing the most does not equate to productivity, and busyness can lead to burnout.

If we find ourselves maintaining an unsustainable pace, staying busy but not necessarily purposeful, it's time to reimagine our leadership. We don't want to continue operating at an untenable pace lest we start leading on empty. When we're on empty, we are too prone to miss God for our assignments, our relationships suffer, and we end up operating on fumes. That's not healthy. (I'll say more about my experiences with leading on empty in chapter 3.)

Stretching Limits

The Samaritan woman's patience with this stranger always strikes me as interesting. No doubt she came to the well to get the water she needed for the day's household chores. She had meals to prepare and clothes to wash, and the day was already half gone.

Yet she took the time to talk with Jesus.

Unfortunately, we sometimes miss the invitation to sit with Jesus because we are stretched to the limit and miss the prompting to move purposefully in a new direction. We have only so much time each day and throughout our lives to do what really matters. Yet we heap upon ourselves unreasonable expectations to try to do everything and be everything to everyone. We stretch limits as if they are elastic bands. But those limits are the naturally occurring circumstances in our lives that set constraints on what we can do, how much we can do, and how frequently we can do these things before they'll hinder our mental, emotional, or physical health.

Though I never want to be limited in my thinking, I recognize naturally occurring limits are our God-given friends.

For example, there are twenty-four hours in a day, no more and no less. Sister leaders, we need to stop trying to cram twenty-five hours of work into one day, ignoring biological, relational, and recharging needs. When we continually stretch the limits in our lives, we experience chronic stress and eventually become overwhelmed. We can't lead well in that state.

We also face other limits.

Aging is a limit. As we traverse each decade, we slow down a little. The pace we kept at twenty-five is not the same pace most of us can keep at forty-five or sixty-five. It's not just about growing older; it's about growing in wisdom and learning to do things smarter.

Time and space are limits. Each of us can be in only one place at one time. We must stop overcommitting, adding multiple engagements to the same spot in our calendars, and sitting in on two Zoom calls simultaneously. Overcommitting ultimately serves to disappoint others and heaps guilt upon us.

Death is another limit. I suppose it is the ultimate earthly limit; we have only so much time in this world to make a difference. We must be mindful of fully living out our purpose and passion daily to avoid getting mired in the "stuff" that distracts and detracts us from leading a life of significance.

Now that we've looked at why we might need a change, let's reimagine our leadership so we can focus on leading well.

The Power of Reimagining

Imagination is a gift. It is the ability to perceive or see beyond our five senses. To reimagine is to imagine something again but in a different, better way. Reimagining is an ongoing process of visioning, creating, and recasting. In this case, reimagining is visioning, creating, and recasting our leadership to serve our whole lives better. Reimagining our leadership allows us to create a plan for leading well that encompasses our full beings.

The story of the woman at the well is powerful, as it shows Jesus in dialogue with an unnamed woman and reveals the power of the Holy Spirit in our lives. Their interaction leads to a reimagining of salvation as an eternally flowing, life-giving relationship that bubbles up like a spring of fresh water within rather than a rigid set of rules to follow. Their interaction shifts our perspective on worship to an authentic means of accessing the Spirit not to be confined to a place.

Further, this woman's story didn't stop at the end of John 4. The Orthodox Christian tradition's gift is naming this previously unnamed woman as early missionary leader St. Photini. Their chronicling of her legendary story helps us reimagine the woman at the well even further. (I'll share more about her legendary life after the Gospels in chapter 10.)

The same thing is possible for us. We can reimagine our lives and leadership and chronicle our legendary stories for our wellbeing and those we lead and serve. These Orthodox church historians, known as *hagiographers*, had a framework anchored in the oral tradition of recounting and passing down these sacred stories of the faith.[3] To reimagine our leadership, we, too, need a framework, one that prioritizes a wholistic view. We can find one in 1 Thessalonians 5:23: "Now may the God of peace make you holy in every way, and may your whole spirit and soul and body be kept blameless until our Lord Jesus Christ comes again."

This prayer asks the God of peace to make us holy in every way. To be holy is to be set apart for God's purposes. As Christian women, we can connect holiness with wholeness, in that holiness is not a set of dos and don'ts for us to follow but a journey of becoming whole and healthy in our spirit, soul, and body as we draw closer to God. I also believe holiness and wholeness entail receiving and experiencing the peace of God.

This passage deals with the sanctification of the believer, and its emphasis on the whole person being set apart for God's purposes is instructive for us as Christian leaders. The framework we need must address our whole being, not just one dimension of ourselves.

Too often, leadership development frameworks are about developing competencies, which are more cognitive or mental skill sets that guide behavior. Sometimes they include emotional intelligence. But until we address the whole being within the context of our leadership, we won't be able to lead well. The Leading Well Framework (see Figure 1) entails our whole being—spirit, soul, and body. It includes the following nine interconnected dimensions of wellbeing that are particularly relevant for Black women leaders.

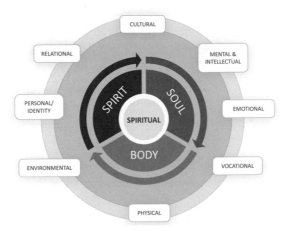

Figure 1: The Leading Well Framework

Spiritual. Spirituality means different things for different people, and we often hear people say "I'm spiritual, not religious." When I speak of *spiritual*, I am referring to the inner life or heart from which flows what we say and do. Our spirituality is the core dimension of leadership wellness for Black women of faith. When we're filled with the Spirit of God, it is from that spiritual wellspring that wisdom, revelation, and insight for all other dimensions of our lives flow. It is from this spiritual core that we access the well of living water to discern what is needed and possible for every other dimension of our lives. Can we imagine what our lives and leadership would look like if we truly led from the well?

Personal identity. We must be clear and confident in who we are. We need to embrace who we are in Christ! We also need clarity on how we can be our full selves in various contexts. As Black Christian leaders, we have often been challenged to assimilate into someone else's sense of who we should be. To lead well means we must be able to show up as authentically Black and woman, faithful followers of Christ, and connected to a community.

Relational. Leadership is about relationships, because a leader-follower framework creates a relational connection. The quality of those relationships affects the quality of our leadership. We are relational beings, and our relationships serve our ability to thrive—or not. To lead well, we need healthy social interactions inside and outside our professional contexts. And as leaders, it is imperative we understand our relationship to our leadership contexts.

Cultural. Connecting to our cultural heritage strengthens our ability to lead. The values of justice and service inform our leadership. Leading well entails identifying with and honoring our cultural heritage and creatively expressing our cultural connection. Micah 6:8 reminds us, "[God] has shown you, O [woman], what *is* good; And what does the LORD require of you But to do justly, To love mercy, And to walk humbly with your God?" (NKJV). Informed by our culture, in humility, we lead from a service-orientation and by making a more just and equitable world. In other words, our leadership is not self-centered or me-oriented. There's more to it than just getting the bag for ourselves!

Mental and intellectual. Our mindset and thinking patterns are critical to leading well. Leadership can challenge us to grow. It can also enable us to facilitate growth in others. What we think shapes what we do. If stinking thinking prevails, we will lead from a place of insecurity, with a critical spirit, and/or through mistrust by micromanaging our teams. If we think, *The whole world is against me*, we will lead from a place of suspicion, second-guessing our teams and putting systems in place that undermine teamwork and efficiency. Such mindsets and thinking patterns wreck individuals—and environments. But by embracing the promise of a sound mind found in 2 Timothy 1:7, we can lead with confidence, through clear communication, by and through grace, and from an empathetic framework that uplifts and builds teams and environments.

Emotional. Mental and emotional health are integrally connected. Being able to express our emotions in healthy ways in our leadership roles is essential to being personable and productive. Like the psalmist, we can thank God for making us "so wonderfully complex!" (Ps. 139:14). Our emotionality is a part of that complexity and serves us in our leadership.

Vocational. Vocational wellness ensures we live out our leadership as a sense of calling, not compulsion, and from an awareness of opportunity, not a mere obligation. When we lead vocationally, we can see our careers as a series of callings in which we live out our God-given purpose in service to others. Vocational wellbeing also includes stewardship of the resources attained through our work, finances, and experiences.

Physical. We've each been given one body and must become a steward of that one body from which we lead. Our physical wellbeing entails caring for our body in terms of getting rest, paying attention to what and how we eat, and doing physical activity.

Environmental. Environmental wellbeing deals with the place and space in which we lead, work, and live. The environmental dimension of wellness for us also includes identifying the areas in which we feel our most authentic selves. Sometimes that is getting outdoors in nature, and it includes creating peaceful spaces in our homes.

All these factors are important to our ability to lead well. Considering them will help us clarify the current state of our leadership and then reimagine what could be.

Strategic Times for Reimagining

In my coaching practice, I have found there are strategic times and seasons of life when we may need to reimagine our leadership. During times of vocational transition, such as changing jobs or careers, or after a promotion, we can create something new. With every major life change, such as marriage, divorce, childbirth, adoption, or becoming a caregiver for elderly loved ones, we may need to adjust our rhythms, routines, and practices to thrive and to lead well. Such changes demand we assess and adjust our leadership for our souls' sakes.

While launching a business, we can develop strategic plans that include leadership self-care. Finally, as we get closer to retirement, we must reimagine our next leadership stage with the view that as Black Christian women of faith we will still be vital to our communities. Any or all of these strategic times may cause external pressures, but we can lead well from the inside out.

In the section below, we will begin developing our plan to lead well—reimagining how leadership could look for us when we lead with our wholistic framework in mind. Now is the time to reimagine how we will attend to our wellness while ensuring the health of our business, our role, our further education, and the people we lead. Now is the time to consider the boundaries we need to establish and maintain that will enable us to lead well for the long haul.

Now is the time to prioritize caring for ourselves while leading others.

LEADING WELL REFLECTION QUESTIONS

1. Think about how you lead and your results. What is your "why"—the most important reason—for shifting how you lead?

2. As a Black woman leader in spaces that are not always welcoming, what leadership practices have you adopted to survive? How have these practices affected your wellbeing?

LEADING WELL PRACTICE: REIMAGINING

Spend some time writing your reflections on the following in your journal (or notebook or electronic document).

First, reimagine your leadership. Prayerfully envision leading in a way that prioritizes your wellbeing as a Black woman leader. What might your reimagined leadership look like? What would be different? How do you want to show up in this reimagined space? How might leading in this manner positively affect you and those you lead? Use the Leading Well Framework below and the questions for each of the leading well dimensions.

Second, consider creating a vision board with a picture or image for each dimension. Place your vision board in a location to remind you of your reimagined leadership.

Leading Well Framework

Leading Well Dimension	Prompts to Help You Reflect and Reimagine Your Leadership
Spiritual	What is a nonnegotiable spiritual activity that you must be able to engage in regardless of where you lead? How might reimagined leadership help you more fully express and live out your spirituality in your leadership context?
Personal/ Identity	To lead well means we must be able to show up as authentically Black and woman and faithful followers of Christ. What does this statement mean to you? How would you envision living this out in your current or future leadership role?
Relational	If you could reimagine your relationships with people you lead, what might they look like? What are your current assumptions about relating to people you lead? What new patterns would you adopt to help you and others flourish in those relationships?

Leading Well Dimension	Prompts to Help You Reflect and Reimagine Your Leadership
Cultural	What might your leadership look like if you could truly draw upon the strength of your culture without being boxed in by other cultural assumptions that may no longer work for you?
Mental/ Intellectual	What would intellectual fulfillment look like in your reimagined leadership? How will you support or protect your mental health? What would be crucial for your mental wellbeing in this reimagined space? How would you be able to express your creativity?
Emotional	What leadership context can you imagine enabling you to take the mask off and show your authentic self without fear of being discounted or minimized? What leadership context do you desire that would allow you to experience and express joy, hopefulness, and delight?
Vocational	To whom or what do you feel called? What causes are you compelled to serve? What skills, abilities, gifts, and experiences give insight into your vocation?
Physical	What would be your ideal pace and focus on your reimagined leadership space? How would this reimagined role facilitate the care of your body?
Environmental	What is your ideal workplace? What does it look, feel, or sound like? How does it make you feel before you get there, while you are there, and after you leave?

As you read each chapter and conduct the end-of-chapter activities, you can gain greater insight into these dimensions of wellbeing for yourself. I encourage you to come back to what you've written in response to the prompts in the above Leading Well Framework and update your responses according to the new insights you gain as you journey through this book.

At the end of the book is a guide to putting your leading well plan in place using all the information you have gathered and reflected on. Ready? Let's go!

TWO

AFFIRM YOUR IDENTITY

I am a Samaritan woman.

John 4:9

A few years ago, I led an all-day leadership development workshop for a company during Women's History Month. During the break, several women, including a younger white woman I'll call Casey, came to the platform to talk with me. At some point in my presentation, I referred to my age, and Casey wanted to attest that I did not look my age, similar to most Black women she knew.

"Before my corporate job," she said, "I used to be a makeup artist, and after doing makeup for African American women, I know Black don't crack!" Some other white women around us laughed nervously; others just stared, unsure what to make of that comment.

Casey was from the South, and she punctuated her words with just the right flair in her gestures and inflection in her tone to let me know she had indeed spent enough time around Black women to feel she had earned the right to use this cultural expression.

As Black women reading this book, I am sure most of us are familiar with this phrase from our community. "Black don't crack" is *our* expression that bears witness to the tendency for many Black women to retain beautiful skin with minimal wrinkles as we age. I attribute it to the melanin in our skin that serves as a protective shield from damaging sunrays.

I was somewhat amused at Casey's appropriation of a phrase from Black culture, though it also felt overly familiar. Despite how surprised I was by her words, they did make me think about the areas where Black *does* crack.

On my leadership journey, I've discovered that as Black women leaders, we'll crack from the inside out if we are not careful. We'll look gorgeous on the outside while we unconsciously absorb the almost daily blows of bias and barriers. We'll crack mentally, physically, emotionally, and spiritually and still carry on as if we are unfazed by the systemic racism we regularly encounter. But over time, those cracks will negatively impact our health, our relationships, our leadership, and those we serve.

That's why it is imperative we understand the importance of developing a healthy leadership identity to mitigate the effects of bias and barriers we face every day.

Leading through Adversity

Black women's leadership is often steeped in adversity because we are often working in places where microaggressions and biases thrive. Statistics bear this out. In a 2015 report published by the Center for Talent Innovation, Black women were more likely than white women to report feeling stalled (44 percent vs. 30 percent) and that their talents weren't recognized by their superiors (26 percent vs. 17 percent).[1]

A 2019 report also published by the Center for Talent Innovation revealed that Black employees experience a great deal of prejudice at work, namely in the form of microaggressions.[2] Workplace cultures rife with exclusion and microaggressions are harmful to employees and decrease their engagement in the organization. Through research conducted by my consulting company, it's clear that such workplaces also can negatively impact the overall well-being of Black women leaders.

Awareness of what a microaggression is—and is not—has increased in recent years. Journalist Elizabeth Hopper provides a succinct definition of *microaggression*: it is a "subtle behavior—verbal or nonverbal, conscious or unconscious—directed at a member of a marginalized group that has a derogatory, harmful effect. Chester Pierce, a Black psychiatrist at Harvard University, first introduced the term in the 1970s."[3] Dr. Derald Wing Sue, a Chinese American researcher, created a means of categorizing microaggressions that has been very helpful in understanding both racial and gender microaggressions.[4]

Microaggressions are often directed against Black women due to implicit bias and/or ignorance. They are seemingly small assaults on a person's humanity based on their identity. But Black women know there is nothing "micro" about such actions or their impact. These actions might include being told, "I don't see you as a Black woman, just as a woman," or "You're pretty for a Black girl." These comments attempt to minimize our Blackness and invalidate our identity. Another microaggression might be the comment, "You are *so* articulate." It always comes across as if the speaker has very low expectations for Black women to be able to string together verbs and nouns.

For Black women, our hair can also reveal common workplace biases, causing some to minimize our professionalism, competence, and leadership. I remember when I was making the journey to go natural and intentionally had a conversation about this transition with my top client, whose business represented well over 60 percent of my company's revenue. It's ludicrous now to think that I felt the need to ensure that my clients would not underrate my competence and hamper my company's success based on my kinky hair pattern.

45

Hair-based biases are so prevalent they have sparked new legislation. The CROWN (Create a Respectful and Open World for Natural Hair) Act was created in 2019. First passed in California, it aims "to ensure protection against discrimination based on race-based hairstyles by extending statutory protection to hair texture and protective styles such as braids, locs, twists and knots in the workplace and in schools."[5]

In talking with Black women leaders, I know these instances of bias and exclusion leave many of us feeling undervalued, insecure, embarrassed, disrespected, and even rejected. We cloak our sadness and anger and suit up to handle our business for another day. But beneath the veneer, cracks occur.

As consultant and author Mary-Frances Winters writes in *Black Fatigue*:

> Whether we work in an entry-level job or have made it into leadership, our identities as Black women shape narratives that are very different from those of other identity groups. For example, stereotypes that Black women must overcome in the workplace include being aggressive, opinionated, and angry.[6]

The aim of *Leading Well* is not to document all the disparities experienced by Black women. But a few statistics remind us of the toll our bodies pay for leading while Black and woman.

- From 1999 to 2020, the death rate of Black working age women[7] was 47 percent higher than that of white women, 44 percent higher than Native American women, and 201 percent higher than that of Asian or Pacific Island women.[8]
- Over a decade ago, scientists explored a link between stress and aging in Black women, finding that "at ages 49–55, black women are 7.5 years biologically 'older' than white women" because of stress-induced aging.

"Indicators of perceived stress and poverty" accounted for 27 percent of this difference, they found.[9]

- Black women are three times more likely to die during childbirth than white women in the United States, according to a review presented at the American Diabetes Association's 80th Scientific Sessions.[10]

- According to *The Root* journalist Lottie L. Joiner, "extreme stress causes wear and tear on our internal organs, contributing to heart disease, high blood pressure and stroke in black women—all diseases of aging."[11]

- Joiner adds, "The cumulative impact of overexposure to stress hormones takes a toll on the body and contributes to the development or progression of such ailments as cardiovascular disease, obesity, diabetes, susceptibility to infection, carcinogenesis, and accelerated aging."[12]

- Finally, according to the Black Women's Health Imperative, the 2020 pandemic and COVID-19 "highlighted the racial, ethnic, and socioeconomic inequities experienced by communities of color [and the] pandemic has further entrenched the health inequalities faced by Black women."[13]

The above data reveal, as many of us know intuitively, that Black women carry a heavy load. Think about it. Most of us are raised to be strong. We are taught to work hard to prove ourselves in a world that is still rife with stereotypes we must resist every day of our lives. We grit our teeth and hold in our true feelings lest we get labeled an angry Black woman for speaking too forthrightly.

We take care of so many people around us, and too often we don't take care of ourselves. Even the most privileged among us seem to fall prey to stress overload. In other words: leading while Black and woman is costly to our sense of self.

Yet as Black women of faith, we can develop strategies for mitigating the effects of these biases. That's why it is crucial for us to understand the agency or personal power that comes with our identity in Christ and our cultural heritage.

Maintaining a healthy perspective of our identity amid bias, stereotypes, and negative narratives requires accepting the imago Dei (the image of God in us), internalizing our authentic identity in Christ, understanding the dynamics of bias, and affirming cultural traditions that strengthen our agency.

Accepting the Imago Dei

The woman at the well told Jesus, "I am a Samaritan woman." She knew who she was in that pivotal moment—and boldly affirmed her identity.

Before we revisit their conversation, let's remember that the story of God's relationship with us starts at the very beginning of creation. Genesis 1:27 declares, "So God created human beings in [God's] own image."

It is a familiar verse, but let it sink in.

We are created in the image of God.

This verse is foundational to the doctrine of imago Dei that posits because humans are created in God's image, we bear a likeness to God in our very essence that has implications for how we see ourselves and others—how we respect ourselves and others.

God's act of creating us in God's image speaks of a special connection between humanity—in all our diverse array—and divinity. Because of our makeup, we bear the likeness of God in our ability to think, plan, and actualize; to love, care, and have compassion.

And here's the truth worth embracing: when God created us, as Black women, we were created in God's image. Our being is sacred space, as we are repositories of the image of God. We must remind ourselves and each other that we are "fearfully and wonderfully made" in the image of God (Ps. 139:14 NKJV).

Contrary to a white supremacist twist on Christianity, no one ethnic group has a monopoly on the physical likeness of God. As Jesus told the Samaritan woman, "God is Spirit" (John 4:24). We bear God's likeness in the totality of our whole being. Whether your skin is mahogany, café au lait, caramel, or almond; your hair is kinky, curly, or straight; your lips are thin or full; your eyes brown or gray—you are created in the image of God, equal with every other human being on this planet. Your very being is God's handiwork (Eph. 2:10).

Humans separated from God's divine will for creation constructed racist systems that put people groups in a hierarchy, deeming some groups (white Europeans) more important and valuable than others. That was *never* God's intent. But racism and misogyny work overtime trying to make us believe otherwise. Consequently, those false beliefs about ourselves affect everything about our lives, including our leadership.

One Black woman leader I know is a case in point. Growing up, she had been told time and again by a parent that she was "so black." The parent meant this as a negative quality, and this woman became self-conscious of her dark brown skin. That parent had bought into European aesthetics as the standards for beauty, a form of internalized racism. Consequently, because this woman was not confident in her looks, she often overcompensated in her leadership role by striving to be overprepared and have all the right answers. Rather than accept her inherent worth in the skin she was created in, she contrived other outward ways of trying to make herself valuable. Such external measures are never firm foundations for our worth and dignity.

Jesus came to reveal God's love and restore us to God. That truth of being created in God's image is the firm foundation upon which we can stand as beautiful Black women upon our inherent worth. Accepting the imago Dei, each of us can confidently affirm, *I am a Black woman created in God's image, worthy of respect and dignity.*

Internalizing God's Love

Many of us hail from a lineage of enslaved ancestors who worked for everything. They had to. Whether in the fields or the big house, they were forced to work hard just to stay alive within the evils of slavery and gendered racial oppression. Work became a part of their identity and a part of their cultural values in a dehumanizing system. This culture helped them survive.

I see culture as the system of shared beliefs and values, passed down from generation to generation, which shapes the identity of a people and helps them survive in their environment.

The primacy of work—labor taking first place over everything else—was one of those values passed down for generations in so many of our families. So much so that, if you are like me, it is also central to our relationship with God. My identity as a Black woman of faith also centered around working to prove my worth.

Serving God as an outgrowth of our faith is a biblical principle (James 2:14–26). However, too many people mistakenly link salvation with works. I sure did. In fact, early in my Christian walk I believed I had to work to maintain my salvation, so I labored hard to please God. I worked in the church, leading ministry groups as a teenager and young adult. Later, I overworked as a young corporate consultant. And because it was such a part of me, I even worked for love in my relationships.

Do you know how exhausting it is to work *so* hard?

My understanding of work and salvation changed during one transformative season in my life when I relocated to Chicago and became a member of a church where the pastor, Bishop Arthur Brazier, taught so clearly about the transforming grace of God that the related truths permeated every fiber of my being.

Grace is the outworking of God's love for us. God does the work of demonstrating unconditional love so we don't have to.

Before telling the story of Jesus and the Samaritan woman, the apostle John proclaimed God's love for humankind. He affirmed that Jesus did not come into the world to condemn the world but so that people might be saved through Jesus (John 3:16–17). I can't help but believe that Jesus's love for all of humanity compelled him to go through Samaria and engage in a conversation with that Samaritan woman.

God loves humanity in all our diversity. Regardless of how others may see us, God loves us. The anchoring of our identity in the love of God is phenomenally transforming for us—and, by extension, for the people we lead!

After receiving my pastor's sermons and teachings, I finally began to understand grace. No, I'm not sure I will ever *fully* understand grace, but I sure received it. I now embrace it.

Grace *is* God's unconditional love and unmerited favor. I recognized and accepted the love of God, acknowledging there was nothing I could do to earn God's love or to cause God to love me any more or less.

Bottom line: I realized I could stop working for something I already had. I didn't need to prove my worth. I just needed to grasp and internalize who I was in Christ. Thanks to my newfound understanding, I began to see myself and others differently.

I began to see my role as a leader differently too. I came to view it as a God-ordained calling. (We'll explore leadership as a vocation or calling in chapter 8.) As a change agent, I could use my leadership role as a vehicle to help effect change and transform systems burdening Black women.

God's love is transforming. That is why we can affirm, *I am a Black woman loved by God.*

That affirmation is also transforming.

Understanding the Dynamics of Bias

What we face as Black women in many leadership contexts is not new. I am not minimizing our issues, but it is important to understand that so much of what we face because of who we are stems from the vestiges of sinful historical racism and misogyny.

Thanks be to God: historical bias does not stop the Lord from managing within these systems and ultimately equipping more of us to challenge and change them.

Case in point: the woman at the well's encounter with Jesus. Even the most cursory perusal of Scripture reveals the historical tensions between the Samaritans and the Jewish people. When Jesus showed up on what I imagine to be a bright sunny day at high noon, he did not or could not mistake the woman's ethnicity and gender as he requested a drink of water. Jesus was aware of the tension between the Samaritans and the Jewish people. In fact, Jesus used his teaching to cast Samaritans in a favorable light, challenging the stereotypes of his people. (The parable of the Good Samaritan in Luke 10:25–37 is an example.)

I'm sure we can relate to this type of interracial/interethnic strife. We experience it today in the United States and other nations where the tensions of historic racial divides still linger. In nineteenth-century America, the issue of whether women, men, and children of African ancestry should be enslaved split the nation apart as Southern states seceded from the Union. Following the Union's victory in the Civil War, legislation solidified the citizenship and rights of Black people on paper.

We know from US history—and our present-day lived experiences—that those rights were not fully enacted or enforced. Years of Jane and Jim Crow segregation prevented Black people from fully realizing equal rights. Even after the Civil Rights Movement and the more recent movements for gender and racial justice, race- and gender-based biases persist and are evident in disparities in health care, education, and workplace advancement, among other areas.

Racism *is* systemic.

Israel's history also included a civil war of sorts. The book of 2 Kings chronicles a once unified nation being divided into two kingdoms. The northern kingdom, Israel, established its capitol in Samaria. Eventually, the Assyrian nation overran the northern kingdom. The leaders of Assyria relocated people of various nations to Samaria, where they settled in with the majority Israelite population. The Israelites in Samaria intermarried with these relocated people. To maintain a version of their religion, they established temple worship in Samaria, on Mt. Gerazim, near Shechem. Northern kingdom leaders empowered their residents to worship locally and not make the trek to Jerusalem for the feast and festival days. That was a big no-no for the leaders of the southern kingdom.

The Samaritans used a religious text that consisted of only the first five books of the Law, known as the Pentateuch, that had minor deviations from the accepted Hebrew text of the Jews.[14] These differences created animosity between the two nations, evidenced in the New Testament. The animosity ran deep on both sides for generations.

When Jesus asked the woman at the well for a drink of water, he broke with cultural tradition, crossing over ideological and cultural boundaries that had kept the two people groups separated for hundreds of years. But that's how our Lord is.

The biases and prejudices of people do not constrain the Lord. And cultural traditions or systems that limit leadership to one gender or privilege one cultural or racial group over another do not affect God's leadership choices.

That's why we can affirm, *I am a Black woman equipped to lead wherever God chooses.*

Asserting Agency

Listen to our Samaritan sister at the well. Knowing the Jewish man standing before her was breaking cultural tradition, she became curious about his intentions. Her response to Jesus's request for water was, "You are a Jew, and I am a Samaritan woman. Why are you asking me for a drink?" (John 4:9).

In making the implicit in the scenario explicit, she asserted her own identity and, therefore, her agency or power. Jesus needed something from her (a drink of water), and she immediately established the terms of the engagement by inquiring into this man's motives for violating cultural boundaries and approaching her.

She did not yet know his identity.

She recognized that a Jewish stranger sat by Jacob's well, a site her culture held in reverence, asking her for a drink of water. They both knew that in those days, Jewish people would not have shared a drinking "fountain" with Samaritans, not unlike some people of my grandmother's day in the southern United States. And quite frankly, the Samaritans held similar biases against Jewish people.

When she asserted, "I am a Samaritan woman," in essence, she was saying, "In this place, in this space, who I am means something. In this space, I have the power to respond or not." Agency is about our power to choose.

She then turned the tables and chose to ask him a question. "Why are you asking me for a drink?" (v. 9). When we speak up—even if *just* to ask a question—we resist forces attempting to silence or erase us.

Sisters, you know that asking questions in a male-dominated space is a power play. There is power in asking questions that cause others to stop and think about their words and actions toward us. There is power in asking questions of other leaders to start a conversation that can lead to real change. There is power in asking questions that spark personal reflection concerning agency, moving us more in line with our God-given identity and calling.

By asserting her agency, the woman at the well opened the door to a fuller conversation. The best part of this story is that Jesus already knew who she was and was not thrown off by her questioning. Instead, he spoke with her about a "drink"—an invitation to a relationship with God empowered by the Spirit—that would shift her thinking and life.

So it is with us as Black women of faith. The Lord knows *us*.

God knows who we are and has given us something to shift our thinking and life so that other people's biases do not constrain us.

What is it? At the deepest level of agency is our power to affirm, *I am a Black woman empowered by God.*

That affirmation carries the truth of who we are and what we possess. We have the ability to respond based on our inherent worth and identity. You see, asking a powerful, well-timed question enables us to not react on autopilot but to get the information we need to respond with intentionality. That's how questions are empowering; they enhance our ability to respond. We retain the power to choose.

Asking a question may seem simple, but asking the right question at the right time is one of the most powerful things we can do. There will be many times when people violate boundaries around us or say something about us that seems off. If we're not careful, their actions can tend to put us on the defensive and even tempt us to act out of character.

Instead, when confronted with bias while leading, we have some choices. Yes, we can ignore it, overlook it, and do nothing. Or we can ask some questions, thus using our God-given power.

- To the person who makes an offhanded, microaggressive comment that feels offensive: "What did you mean by that? Can you help me understand?"
- To the HR department: "What policies are in place to mitigate the bias Black women experience in this workplace?"
- To an organization's leadership: "How do I get involved in our DEI efforts? What are you doing to attract, develop, retain, and advance more Black women into leadership?"
- To ourselves: "Am I celebrated and respected here, or am I merely tolerated? What are my options? Who do I need to talk with to create options?"

There is power in asking questions. *Sister leaders, we can claim our power. We can assert agency as we lead.*

Identifying with the Culture

When the woman at the well said to Jesus, "I am a Samaritan woman," she not only asserted her agency but her connection to her community and culture. In doing so, she identified with the history of her people, the heritage of her people, and the values, beliefs, and stories that anchored her people.

When Jesus offered to give her living water, she challenged him. "Are You greater than *our* father Jacob who gave us the well?" (John 4:12 NKJV, emphasis added). Jacob's well was a community marker for her culture. Here she quickly identified with and touted the patriarch Jacob, who was revered by her people. We know we draw strength from our cultures as well as experience stressors because of our cultural identities.[15]

Jacob's well was a signpost of her heritage, in which she was deeply steeped. In another verse, she proclaims that "*our* ancestors" worshiped on that mountain (v. 20, emphasis added). Our cultures shape our identities.

To proclaim she was a Samaritan woman said something about her cultural identity, as both Samaritan and woman. Being a Samaritan meant something to her, and she conveyed that to this strange man from another culture.

So it is with us as Black women leaders. We hail from a people of overcomers. We hail from a people who passed on the value of kinship, community, and connectedness. We hail from a people who uplift our communities.

Like the Samaritan woman, we can proclaim what our ancestors recognized, respected, and passed on to us so that we never forget who we are as a people. We are knit together by our culture, and faith in God is deeply embedded in our culture.

To be Black women leaders of faith means something. It means we are walking in the paths carved out through our ancestors' prayers, preaching, protesting, and protecting.

> We hail from an overcoming people who survived slavery and segregation.
>
> We hail from overcoming Black women who faced trauma, poverty, sickness, and disease due to systemic racism but *still* fought to keep families together and Black love alive.
>
> We hail from enterprising female business owners whose big ideas and products elevated families and communities.
>
> We hail from overcoming church mothers who prayed, fasted, sang, tithed, *and* cooked up steaming batches of fried chicken to keep church lights on and sanctuary doors open.
>
> We hail from civilly disobedient women who marched, protested, refused to give up their seats, and went to jail to resist injustice and advance civil rights.
>
> We hail from politically savvy women who fought for suffrage and cast votes through the years to *choose* leaders who looked like us or were allies who fought for us.

As we lead today, we continue their legacy of justice and equity. We continue to be overcomers. And whether in the boardroom or mail room, community agency or school, as Black women of faith, we will survive and help each other survive and thrive.

We can, therefore, each proclaim, *I am a Black woman with a godly heritage of overcoming.*

So, sisters, let's affirm our identity in all its complexity. God has created us distinctly, placed us in communities, and loves us individually, collectively, and eternally. God has called and is equipping us to serve from places of authenticity and wholeness. We can and must affirm who we are and that we intend to lead well.

LEADING WELL REFLECTION QUESTIONS

1. How has leading while Black and woman affected your physical, mental, or emotional health? What might you do differently now to lead well despite personal or systemic factors?

2. Think about the last time you used the superwoman persona to handle your business. What did you gain? What did it cost you? What might you do differently next time you feel the need to try to be a superwoman?

LEADING WELL PRACTICE: AFFIRMATIONS

Throughout this chapter, I provided the following five "I am" affirmations:

- I am a Black woman created in God's image, worthy of respect and dignity.
- I am a Black woman loved by God.
- I am a Black woman equipped to lead wherever God chooses.
- I am a Black woman empowered by God.
- I am a Black woman with a godly heritage of overcoming.

Select one of these affirmations. Read it aloud. How do those words sound to you? How do they make you feel? In a journal, write out what that affirmation means for you and your leadership.

After you complete the first, choose another and repeat the activity. Continue until you have written about all five.

THREE

ASK FOR WHAT YOU NEED

Please . . . give me this water!

John 4:15

One day I was speaking with a friend on the phone, process-ing my workload and some new requests. As I talked about my overflowing plate of demands, I casually remarked, "Well, I can do all things through Christ who gives me strength," quoting Philippians 4:13. And my friend pushed back on me just as quickly, responding, "But does Christ want you to do *every*thing?"

My friend's well-timed, powerful question caused me to pause and seriously reflect on my busyness. In a flash of insight, I realized I was really doing too much under the guise of working for Christ.

Many of us think it is a sign of leadership success that we have more work than can be humanly done in twenty-four hours. The Holy Spirit led this friend to ask just the right question to cause me to explore my understanding of what the Lord really wanted me to do. That questioning was the first step to recognizing my need for change.

And more of us need good friends willing to push back on our misappropriation of Scripture, especially that verse I used, to justify our being overworked, overwhelmed, and worn out. Too many of us use Scripture to justify our near burned-out lives, our weary souls, and being stretched way too thin.

That activity level often stems from not wanting or knowing how to ask for the help we need. Quite frankly, being so busy we don't have time for recharging, refueling, and refilling will result in leading on empty.

Leading on Empty

Our bodies are designed for work—and rest! More often than not, we push through to serve others and to meet the expectations of our superiors, teams, coworkers, families, and friends. We shift our personal needs to autopilot in order to respond to the demands placed on our leadership, and as a result we get too busy to listen to the inner working of our souls, which experience pressure and stress. When no reprieve is in sight, our souls cry out, cajole, and challenge us to slow down, to care for ourselves as we care for others, and to recalibrate what we are doing in our leadership.

We all have examples of getting caught up in responsibilities and expectations. Maybe you've been training new staff around the clock, answering emails after hours and on weekends instead of being present with your friends and family. Or maybe you picked up extra responsibilities in your organization until fatigue forced you to take some of those vacation days you had accumulated over the years.

Unfortunately, too often we fail to listen to our souls. Yet we should. In her book *Strengthening the Soul of Your Leadership*, spiritual director Ruth Haley Barton writes,

The soulful leader pays attention to such inner realities and the questions that they raise rather than ignoring them and continuing the charade or judging himself or herself harshly and thus cutting off the possibility of deeper awareness.[1]

Too many of us portray a strong outer image while growing increasingly weary. Concerning spiritual leadership, Barton contends it "emerges from our willingness to stay involved with our own soul—that place where God's Spirit is at work stirring up our deepest questions and longings to draw us deeper into relationship with [God]."[2]

When we don't listen to our souls' deepest stirrings, we give and give until we deplete our inner resources. If we've been leading for any length of time, we've probably experienced this.

The older saints of my faith tradition called this "being dry" or "going through a dry season." During such seasons, we are most prone to reacting harshly to those we lead. We are more likely to feel discouraged in our leadership. When we are dry and unaware, we lead from a jumble of unprocessed emotions. We also expend our inner energy on just getting by and have little energy to truly care, guide, coach, or serve anyone from a life-giving place.

Leading on empty pushes us to the brink of burnout.

With our reserves drained, we have nothing left to give. We try, but it is an impossible mission. During dry seasons, we do not—*cannot*—lead from the vibrant living water mentioned in John 4:15 because we fail to access the living water.

The remedy? Like the Samaritan woman, we must unashamedly ask for what our souls truly need to lead well.

Peter Scazzero describes leaders leading on empty in his book *Emotionally Healthy Leadership*: "In their more honest moments they admit that their cup with God is empty or, at best, half full, hardly overflowing with the joy and love they proclaim to others."[3] When we get to that point of emptiness, we must ask for a refilling. Thankfully, God welcomes—and satisfies—our thirsts.

The Well Within

Jesus offered life-giving water to the woman at the well, and she wanted it. She requested it. Jesus also offered a thirst-quencher: the Holy Spirit. When we draw from the Spirit, we are refreshed, empowered, and equipped to handle the demands of our leadership assignments.

The Samaritan woman's life changed at the well. By consistently drinking from the well that Jesus offers, our lives can change too. We've got to want it—it's available for the asking.

Within communities, wells are essential sources of water for bathing, drinking, cooking, and other everyday activities. Vital in biblical days, they remain crucial in the United States and abroad. Well water must also be available and easily accessible. A full well attracts attention, but the quality of its water determines its usefulness. For drinking or cooking, for example, water is best when it is clean, fresh, and free from poisonous substances.

Just as people still draw water from wells for life's activities, we can draw from the well of the Spirit for spiritual replenishment, energy, and power for daily tasks. Jesus appealed to the Samaritan woman's need and desire for water that fit all these characteristics. He offered her living water from a full well with an endless water supply. She eagerly and thirstily accepted the invitation to drink.

Imagine this woman from the nearby village approaching the community well, perhaps on her daily water run to get what she needed for her household activities. Sitting at the well in the heat of the day was a man, apparently not from her village or culture.

Sweaty, weary, and dusty from his travels, this man needed refreshing from his journey with a drink of water. Yet he had no container, a vital tool for getting his urgent need met. The weary traveler initially asked this woman for a drink. She questioned him. In turn, he offered her a different type of water, living water. Her interest—or skepticism—was piqued.

"'Please, sir,' the woman said, 'give me this water! Then I'll never be thirsty again, and I won't have to come here to get water'" (John 4:15).

She thought the offer was for something wet, liquid, *natural*. However, John 7:37–38 clues us in to its *supernatural* nature. The fountain or wellspring of living water Jesus mentioned and promised this woman was not physical but was the Holy Spirit—an internal gift for guidance promised to every follower of Christ.

The book of John also tells us how the Holy Spirit is crucial to the life of *every* believer. The Holy Spirit

- is *the* agent of the new birth (3:6–8).
- abides with believers forever (14:16).
- is the Spirit of truth (14:17; 15:26; 16:13).
- is the Helper, *the* Comforter who walks alongside us and brings back the teachings of Jesus to our remembrance (14:26; 15:26).
- will not speak on own authority but will tell us only what has been heard from Jesus (16:13).
- guides believers into truth (16:13).
- tells believers things to come (16:13).
- will glorify Jesus and will declare what has been received from Jesus (16:14).
- convicts the world of sin, righteousness, and judgment (16:8).
- empowers us to forgive (20:23).

With all these themes on the works of the Spirit in the Gospel of John, it strikes me as interesting that in the heat of that day at the well, Jesus shared none of them. Instead, Jesus summarized the Spirit's power as *living* water. While trying to get his own human thirst met, he used the image of life-giving water to talk about the Spirit with a woman who would one day become a leader in her own right.

As a leader, she would need the Spirit. The flow of the Spirit revives and refreshes us so that we can lead from a place of wisdom and strength. Like the woman at the well, people are thirsty for the living water that does not disappoint. They want to know their leaders are providing clear—not contaminated—direction, guidance, and oversight.

As Black Christian women, we'll never be free from making mistakes or needing to be replenished, but we have a well from which to draw wisdom and to point people to as the only source that can truly quench their desires.

But when we are dry, don't have the tools, or don't take the time to access what is within, we find ourselves leading on empty. The spiritually dehydrating result is burnout, fatigue, career dissatisfaction, illness, or other detrimental effects on our whole being. Those greatly contrast with the beneficial effects we experience when we lead from wholeness.

When we prioritize our wellbeing and maintain a rhythm of spending regular time at the well, we stay spiritually hydrated. From the Spirit's overflow, we can access the peace of God more readily despite the incessant and sometimes conflicting demands around us.

The spiritually hydrating result of wholistic leadership is better alignment between mind, body, and spirit. We get guidance on managing the stressors in our lives and show up more even-keeled in various situations. Sisters, when we tend to our spiritual, physical, mental, and emotional health, we feel better. We look better. We move better. We even sleep better! When we consistently drink from the well, we can experience an inner peace, despite what may seem like chaos around us.

Ask for Peace

For me, peace is at the heart of leading well. I seek and wait for the peace of God when making decisions. I protect the peace in my home and my work. But there was a time when I had so much going on internally I couldn't even recognize inner peace and didn't know how to ask for it.

After I finished graduate school, I relocated to Chicago to start my new job as a university professor. I knew in my heart that I was supposed to be in Chicago. And I loved teaching! I loved the interaction with students, especially the young Black women who gravitated toward me. I was one of only a handful of Black female professors with whom they got to interact.

Yet other dynamics in my academic department troubled me. One was my salary. My tenure track professorship was impressive but didn't pay what I thought I needed to live in metro Chicago. (I know: one doesn't go into teaching for the money!)

Departmental dynamics and politics also stressed me out. Administrators expected all professors to teach, research, and provide service to the university by serving on various committees. I bristled at the service assignments given to me, thinking that I could better use that time to prepare for classes or gain consulting gigs. And I didn't ask for help in getting acclimated to my new academic world. Sometimes we try to push through the unfamiliar on autopilot by using what is familiar to us. But without developing new strategies, the pressure builds.

So I resigned the second year and went back to what I knew. I accepted a position as a manager of organizational development for a telecommunications company, but I felt so conflicted and started my new corporate role feeling guilty about leaving the university.

Then my Dad died one month later after a brief bout with cancer. I was crushed. I had no reserve emotional energy built up.

I had no peace. I needed help.

Members of my old department at the university called, including one who was a former nun. After expressing condolences, she noted my sudden departure from the university.

She ignored my musing when I shared my remorse about leaving and hinted at a desire to return. At that point, I sensed she knew I was in no position to come back to a place I had just left. Instead, she told me a story about a wise mentor who'd often shared with her the importance of walking in peace. "Jeanne, you're not walking in peace," she observed. "You have to walk in peace."

I let those words sink in. I was *not* walking in or leading from a place of internal peace. No wonder I was an emotional mess!

I couldn't drink from the living water Jesus had promised because I couldn't wade through all the stuff blocking me from the well.

Peter Scazzero again helps us to understand this dynamic in his book *Emotionally Healthy Spirituality*. He writes, "Emotional health and spiritual maturity are inseparable."[4] Sometimes we try to separate the two and miss the integral connection between all dimensions of ourselves. "Emotional deficits are manifested by a pervasive lack of awareness. Unhealthy leaders lack, for example, awareness of their feelings, their weaknesses and limits, how their past impacts their present, and how others experience them."[5] Scazzero continues, "Spiritual deficits typically reveal themselves in too much activity."[6] Spiritually unhealthy leaders are so busy doing the work of the Lord that they miss the Lord of the work.

In my case, I had pushed through to complete a doctoral program in record time, relocated to a new city, started an assistant professorship, became active at a new church, landed a few consulting gigs, and maintained a busy speaking schedule. I was emotionally, mentally, and spiritually drained. Superwomen can recognize this pattern.

Hanging up from my call with my former colleague, I made one of the best decisions of my life: I found a counselor and went into therapy.

I encourage everyone reading this book to do the same if peace is elusive or you find yourself perpetually conflicted. The stigma of counseling is slowly fading within our culture. But even if we're in a family or church that frowns upon counseling, we have to be courageous and love ourselves enough to attend to our souls. We have to seek out referrals and make the appointment. By the way, as a business leader, pastor, and coach, even in this season of my life, I regularly see a therapist or other helping professional such as a coach or spiritual director as part of my overall wellness support system.

Leading well includes doing the inner work of self-reflection and gaining the skills and tools to experience and process our feelings and the feelings of others. It means accessing the peace that we "proclaim to others."[7]

I slowed down long enough to meet with a professional who could help me process what was going on inside, then I learned to sit with it. I learned that I had (and still grapple with) perfectionism tendencies that drove me to overperform, overwork, and overfunction, only to get overwhelmed because I sometimes ignored the inner tugs of my soul.

Doesn't that sound like so many of us?

Many Black women of faith have been socialized to overwork and be what Dr. Chanequa Walker-Barnes calls the "StrongBlack-Woman."[8] That's not a typo—she scrunches the three words together to make an important point. With the "literary scrunching" of these three words into one term, she distinguishes between being "a Black woman who is strong" and being a Black woman whose extremes in "caregiving, independence, and emotional strength/regulation" cause her to operate in the world from a superwoman "scripted role."[9]

Many of us were brought up into such a role. We saw our mothers, aunties, grandmothers, and godmothers work hard, sacrifice for their families, and care for others with little time to care for themselves. They put everyone else first. It was just the way it was. They didn't ask for what they needed. And they didn't complain. Instead, they often suffered in silence. Although they meant well, they modeled what it meant to ignore the soul's cry for rest and replenishment.

That is why Dr. Walker-Barnes describes the StrongBlack-Woman as "a legendary figure, typified by extraordinary capacities for caregiving and for suffering without complaint."[10] Such a woman is *not* a leadership ideal.

When we forsake the StrongBlackWoman as a wellbeing goal, we will find it easier to seek and find inner peace. We will be emboldened to ask for what we need and see our needs met. We will also set a different standard for the younger generations who are watching our every move.

Years from now, if we really model leading well, today's young Black girls will be leaders who prioritize relationships over bottom lines, honor Sabbath rests, take sabbaticals, keep a therapist on speed dial, use *all* their vacation time, and play as hard as they work. Wouldn't that be something?

It's time to create new images—for them and us—that prioritize our ability to care for ourselves as leaders and leave a different legacy for the next generation of Christian women leaders. I discuss how to do so in the last chapter of this book.

Ask for the Living Water

The woman of Samaria asked for living water so she could drink from the fountain Jesus mentioned. Remember, we learned that the living water is the Holy Spirit. We, too, can and must ask for living water in our times of need.

How do we access the living water?

First, we stop and get still. For leaders, this can be so difficult. Because we're high functioning and action-oriented, it takes discipline for us to stop and get still. But we must. Just as we schedule daily time to eat and drink natural sustenance, we need to schedule daily time for our spiritual care. For example, I start my day with prayer and devotion and have nightly prayers with my family. These prayer times are bookends in my day.

We should also plan daily downtime in our work schedule. I have one chief executive friend who plans a lunch break daily where she eats by herself and does not check emails. This daily me-time gives her a mental break from the busy demands of the day. When was the last time you enjoyed an electronics-free-only-me lunch break? Perhaps it's time to pull out the planner and schedule at least one of those weekly.

To wrap up the week, we should also have some extended time for being still. For years now, I've been observing a weekly Sabbath. For me, Sabbath-keeping entails taking a break from work and productivity to attend to self-care. It may include times of prayer. I may read a good book or just kick it with my husband. In the past I also watched Lifetime movies with my elderly mom. I sorely miss her and our time together—what sweet, sweet memories! Sabbath time can include anything that brings you delight and enhances your wellbeing. But not work—no work emails, no work calls, no thinking about work. We must break from our work, so our work does not break us. In these times of taking a break from our work, our whole being can be restored, renewed, and reenergized, and our inner self can tune in to the voice of the Spirit.

Second, we breathe. I've started practicing deep breathing to enter prayer time and to regulate the stress in my being. This deep breathing time has become a process of inviting the Spirit to flow through me and expecting the gentle breath of the Spirit to settle me.

In seminary, I learned about a prayer technique called breath prayer. According to author Nancy S. Wiens,

> Breath Prayer appears perhaps as early as the 3rd century. Known as the "Jesus Prayer" or "Prayer of the Heart," it draws from Mark 10:47 where a blind man, Bartimaeus, calls Jesus to heal him. A common form is, "Jesus Christ, Son of God, have mercy on me." By placing a few words on the inhale and a few on the exhale, it unites the prayer with the body.[11]

In this form of prayer, we focus on our breathing. We might say "Jesus" as we inhale and "have mercy on me" as we exhale.

The older Black women of the church I attended in college also had a similar prayer practice, I remember. They were altar workers, ministering women who prayed with people who responded to the call at the end of sermons to seek the Lord. They started praying at the altar but often moved to a prayer room where these women helped the seekers wait on the Holy Spirit.

One ministering woman had a heart full of love for weary, burdened people. They came in broken, needing to experience the living water of the Holy Spirit. She'd lovingly listen and then give them a Scripture about the Holy Spirit upon which to meditate. She also encouraged them to begin to breathe.

"Close your eyes. Open your mouth. And breathe in, breathe out," she'd instruct.

Sometimes the prayer was one word, "Jesus." At other times it was a prayer of gratitude, "Thank you, Jesus." Sometimes it was a praise, such as, "Hallelujah." I didn't realize it then, but she was teaching those seekers to drink from the living water.

When we drink in the Spirit, we begin to quiet the noise within. The more we sit and focus on our breathing and our heartfelt prayer, the more we are able to listen to the thirsty cry of our souls.

When I was a young girl playing at recess, I'd get so thirsty from running and playing kickball and dodgeball on the school's playground that when it was time to come inside, I'd run right to the water fountain before heading to my classroom. I'd stand in line with my classmates, anxiously awaiting my turn to get a drink. When my turn came, I'd drink in gulp after gulp without breathing. Then I'd stop for a moment, come up for air, then put my head back down for another drink until my thirst was satisfied (or it was someone else's turn).

Drinking from the living water is similar. Just as you cannot see the water in the fountain's pipes but trust it will bubble up when you activate the pump, you can trust that although you cannot see the Spirit, the Spirit is with you.

After running around leading, you need to make time to stop, get still, and take a deep drink from the fountain of the Spirit. The Spirit, the eternal breath or *rûah* of God who hovered over the waters of creation, breathes through us.[12] The eternal breath, the *pneuma* of God, blows like a wind gently over our souls to regenerate our hearts (John 3:6–8).[13] This eternal breath, which Jesus breathed upon the disciples, saying, "Receive the Holy Spirit" (20:22), is available to us. When we sit still and drink the living water, I imagine us breathing in the very breath of God as God's breath blows through us, opening our hearts to healing, creativity, and wholeness.

Ask for the Spirit's Help

Sitting still and breathing are two ways to access the Spirit. Another is to ask for the Spirit's help, like Alicia did. Alicia was an assistant vice president in a large urban school district. She recounts that this assignment was one of the most stressful times in her leadership because of the woman she worked for. Yes, sometimes our biggest obstacles come from other women who look like us! Unhealed hurts in our sense of self cause us to hurt others. We've heard the adage "Hurt people hurt people." When it comes to leadership, hurt leaders not only hurt other individuals but organizations and entire systems. We don't want to be those hurt leaders. It's time for healing. We can ask the Spirit for help.

Alicia recounts how difficult it was to work under this leader, so much so that she dreaded going to work. The department had high turnover because many staff members decided they would not deal with this type of leader. Alicia persisted through the stress. Each day Alicia prayed while she was driving to work. One morning she clearly heard the Spirit ask, *Why don't you ask me to help you?* She paused and responded, "Wait a minute, have I not ever asked you for help?" The question she heard that morning caused her to pivot to a life of prayer to get through the day. God began to give her grace to handle everything she had to deal with during that time.

You may be praying, but have you ever remembered to ask the Spirit to help you?

The Holy Spirit is our Helper who walks with us. It is our privilege and promise to ask for help. Too often, as leaders, we are programmed to just do it: handle the issues and deal with the fallout. Or some of us are afraid to ask for fear of being told no or rejected. But as Christians, we have an inner resource from which we can draw. We can ask for help.

Ask for Spiritual Strategy

As Black women leaders, we are accustomed to thinking strategically with respect to program and policies. Too often, spiritually, we forget to ask God for a strategy in addressing our personal situations. One medical crisis taught me to do so.

I was waiting for the technician to return to the room where she'd just given me an ultrasound of my right ovary. When she entered the room with a look of surprise, I knew this follow-up test showed something different from the one I'd had three months earlier. I had a cyst on my right ovary and was scheduled for surgery the following week. This was to be the final ultrasound before the procedure. The tech asked me to get dressed and wait in the office for the doctor to speak with me. Her voice and demeanor dripped with so much kindness that it made me nervous.

The doctor confirmed that something was amiss. In comparing the ultrasounds, she now saw a mass on my ovary that had not been there before. Cysts show up on ultrasounds differently than a mass does. What was supposed to be a simple procedure of removing a cyst turned into concern that I might have ovarian cancer. This white woman doctor, a referral from my primary care physician, was very clinical and matter-of-fact with her diagnosis. She didn't connect with me or try to alleviate my growing concern.

I was shaken to my core.

I had scheduled a strategic planning session for a ministry at my church that evening. While driving down Lake Shore Drive, I called our assistant pastor and canceled the meeting. I needed to get home. Sisters, our health takes priority over our strategy sessions. We must never be afraid to ask for the time necessary to attend to our wellbeing.

I stretched across my bed and went straight to the well when I got home. I prayed intensely. I didn't know what to do with this new information. It came to me during prayer: *Ask for strategy.* And so, I prayed for strategy.

And the Holy Spirit gave me a strategy—to form an intercessory prayer team of five people to join me in praying for my situation. With urgency, I got up from my bed and called each of the five. When I called the fifth person, the only brother, and told him what was going on, he said, "Doc, why don't you call my wife's OB-GYN for a second opinion?" He told me more about his wife's experience with this doctor. He emphasized that this doctor was a Christian, a believing Black woman.

He offered to get her contact info and called me back within minutes with the number. Time was of the essence, as I was scheduled to fly to the West Coast the following day for business. I pondered how quickly I could get in to see her and if I could get an appointment before my scheduled surgery the following week.

It was already after hours, around 6:00 p.m. I called intending to leave a voice mail for the doctor and was shocked: the doctor was not only in after-hours but answered the phone herself. I told her about the referral and brought her up to speed on the ultrasound. She asked how soon I could get in to her, and I let her know that I was leaving for a two-day business trip. She faxed a release form to have my records sent to her office for her review and gave instructions for scheduling an appointment for when I returned.

At my first in-person appointment with this doctor, she spoke with wisdom and grace. She first said she wanted to do a blood test to see if there were markers in my blood for ovarian cancer. She told me this was not a guarantee but could set my mind at ease. That's what I appreciated about this sister leader's approach—she treated the whole woman. Further, I had asked for a strategy, and the Holy Spirit gave me a plan and led me to a doctor with a strategy.

Ultimately, my doctor removed my ovary and provided follow-up care. So strongly did I sense the need to ask the Spirit for guidance in this situation I now make praying strategically a core part of my life and leadership. Like the woman at the well, we can ask for what we need from the well of the Holy Spirit.

We can go to the well of living water as leaders to ask for help, guidance, wisdom, and direction. To lead from the well means that we do not take the Spirit for granted and fail to access the gifts offered by the Spirit. As Black Christian women, we cannot get so busy leading that we fail to access the living water that not only gives life and refreshes us but flows into every other dimension of our lives as we seek wisdom and guidance for those areas.

LEADING WELL REFLECTION QUESTIONS

1. Think of a time you were leading on empty. What did it feel like? What did it cost you?

2. What prevents you from getting still and sitting with what is going on inside you? What support is available to you?

LEADING WELL PRACTICE: BREATH PRAYER

1. Set a timer for five minutes. (Some smartwatches have a breathing app you can use.) Start paying attention to your breathing. Begin to take deep breaths. When we are most stressed, we tend to breathe very shallowly. Inhale slowly through your nose. Exhale slowly through your mouth. Focus on your breathing and your time with the Lord. Imagine that as you breathe in, you are drinking from the Spirit, and as you breathe out, you are releasing toxic thoughts. Continue this for five minutes, either silently or adding a word or phrase such as "Holy Spirit" as you breathe in and "Help me" as you breathe out.

2. Once you complete the activity, write about the experience in your journal. What was it like? How might you make this practice a regular part of your daily routine, gradually increasing your time?

3. Think of a current situation you are facing in your leadership. In your prayer time today, ask the Holy Spirit to guide you to move forward. Write down what you hear. Heed what you hear.

FOUR

DEFY THE BIAS

You certainly spoke the truth!
John 4:18

W e look within and do the inner work to incorporate healthier practices into our leadership. Yet as we pray for strategies for leading well, we must acknowledge the external barriers we face as Black women leaders and the effects of bias on us.

As we saw in chapter 2, for Black women, gender and racial biases are entrenched in places where we lead and manifest in microaggressive comments and macroaggressive actions. If we aren't careful, these can end up affecting our overall wellbeing as we grapple with the biases.

The woman of Samaria faced bias, not just in her day but down through the years, in the interpretation of her story. The telling of her story has been fraught with narrative bias in how commentators, preachers, and teachers have interpreted her story and labeled her. Much of that narrative bias stems from her admission to Jesus that she had no husband. Yet Jesus called that admission truth-telling.

Bias affects how we lead. It hinders our ability to lead well. And it is prevalent in every room we walk into as Black women. Consider these three conversations:

Overheard in a hospital emergency room: "Where is the doctor? Please get him."

Overheard at a corporate board meeting: "I'm looking for the chairman; did he arrive yet?"

Overheard at a table at a restaurant: "Where is the manager? I need him to straighten out this check."

What do all these comments and related requests have in common? In each case, a Black woman was verbally stripped of her leadership by someone's gender and racial bias. A Black woman doctor, board member, and restaurant owner were assumed not to be in charge simply because of being Black and woman.

Every job is honorable and worthy of respect and dignity. Nonetheless, it is maddening when Black women leaders encounter workplaces where they consistently are not afforded the respect given their leadership position, whatever that is. Understanding and accepting the relationship between structural biases (often expressed through work relationships) and our wellbeing is critical. Developing strategies to defy this bias is essential.

On the surface, it seems as if Jesus did not give the woman at the well her kudos, either. Was Jesus biased? Let's see.

After talking about living water on a hot day by a well, Jesus tells the woman of Samaria to go get her husband. When I read that request, it seemed like it came from left field. I often muse, Why did Jesus raise this subject? Was the earthly Jesus steeped in a patriarchal culture and so would not give the woman this gift of living water without her husband being present? As we will see, that was not the case.

Various interpreters have tried to explain his request. One line of thought is that just as Jesus spoke spiritually about the "living water," he was talking symbolically to her about her "husbands." These interpreters argue he was calling out the "false worship" of the Samaritans.[1] Still others believe Jesus used it as an opportunity to shame her.[2] This line of thought suggests that "Jesus uses her 'shameful' unmarried situation as a rhetorical weapon to disarm her and persuade her of his identity."[3] But does he disarm her? Does she not flip the script to focus on him and ultimately lead the conversation to the question of worship, which we will learn in the next chapter is key to accessing the living water?

Jesus knew she'd had five husbands and the man she was now living with was not her husband. So, why did he give her the directive? Could it be his request was a pivot—a test of sorts—to see how she would respond? She told the truth; she had no husband. He then revealed he knew the details of her story.

Sometimes Jesus confronts us with a situation that causes us to reflect on our case and acknowledge what we have and don't have. In those moments, Jesus fills in the blanks and reveals insight about our situation. And in this case, that knowledge of her life revealed more about him than it did about her.

In what situation might Jesus be confronting us in our leadership, challenging us to tell the truth about what we have and don't have? Perhaps we have an excellent title yet don't have peace. Maybe we have a great salary but little time to spend on the things that could enhance our wellbeing and the wellbeing of those around us. Perhaps we have great ideas but do not voice our opinions honestly for fear of being labeled.

Whatever it is, the Lord is asking us to tell the truth about where we are and tell the truth about who we have become in this place. I believe that's what Jesus wanted to pull from the woman at the well—the truth about where she was. Yet generations of preachers and teachers have homed in on her marital status, reducing her to a mere sexual object.

That's what the patriarchal narrative does. As I shared earlier, patriarchy espouses the power of men over women and limits the power of women to lead. *Patriarchy* basically means "the rule of the father" or "ruling father."[4] This system of male domination has become inscribed in the structures, policies, and practices of our society and institutions.

Yet theologian Sandra Schneiders argues that it is even more. She writes that "patriarchy is not merely a system of male domination of females but the institutionalization of an ideology of 'otherness' that interlinks sexism, racism, classism, and other forms of oppression."[5]

Historically, it is an ancient system or structure in which men rule and male leadership is privileged and normative. After generations of women staking claims to leadership and following our God-given calls, we have advanced to the highest levels of leadership in every system despite these opposing forces. Yet the vestiges of patriarchal thinking and assumptions linger.

The patriarchal narrative around the Samaritan woman that was created and maintained for centuries does what controlling narratives are intended to do: articulate and advance a perspective that privileges a particular view of the world. This view is usually held by the dominant group—the group in power—at the expense of some group that does not hold that power or status.

Narratives are scripts supporting a particular worldview. They help those in power hold on to their power. Dominant narratives can be rife with underlying assumptions that, unless questioned, go unchallenged and maintain the status quo. These narratives are part of the conditions that damage our sense of self and hinder us as Black women from leading from our whole selves.

By creating the script around the Samaritan woman's sexuality, labeling her as sexually promiscuous because of her prior relationships, the patriarchy tries to obscure her worthiness in being considered a leader.

Patriarchs—that is, racist and misogynistic power brokers from the slave era on—likewise created scripts for Black women to live by that are unhealthy and damaging to our souls. To reclaim our right and call to lead from our whole selves without apology or assimilation, it takes challenging the patriarchal narrative of Black women's leadership, much as we are doing with the woman of Samaria's story.

The Narrative Bias

Let's look at some of these patriarchal myths constructed about the woman at the well in various commentaries. Because we are affected by them, it is worth taking a few minutes to explore them further. Her previous marriages have been depicted as a "woman's chequered liaisons with men."[6] She's been described as "experimenting with five husbands" and no longer finding "the marriage ritual necessary."[7]

She's also been described as having "a string of five husbands followed by a lover" in a "domestic arrangement [that] was unthinkable" and compared to "evil."[8] Commentators have inaccurately described Jesus as having a "tone of solemn" rebuke in accusing her "of a life of loose morals."[9]

Finally, the Samaritan woman is said to be "no angel," being "mixed up with a wrong crowd," and a "poor woman from Samaria [with] quite a reputation" with whom Jesus has a "lengthy but candid dialogue." In so doing, "he makes her understand that she needs to profess her sins and change her life before she can obtain this life-giving water—grace."[10]

With no evidence from the text, these commentators read into her life and use conjecture to paint a picture of an out-of-control woman. Their commentaries say more about them than they do about her. Jesus did not accuse her or depict her relations as checkered. We know nothing of the crowd she was a part of to judge it as right or wrong. And we see no evidence in this conversation that Jesus promised her living water predicated upon her changing her life.

Of course, we can flip the script and shed additional light to see the woman of Samaria differently when we take into account the culture in which she lived. As far as we can tell from the socio-logical context of the time, she hailed from a patriarchal culture. According to New Testament professor James McGrath,

> Unless Samaritan law was very different from Jewish law, and their culture likewise radically different, there is no possibility that this meant that the woman had divorced five men. In this patriarchal cultural context, a woman who divorced a couple of husbands would not likely be taken as the wife of yet another. Are we to imagine either that several husbands have divorced the woman, or more plausibly, that the woman has been widowed multiple times?[11]

Another New Testament professor, Lynn Cohick, gives fur-ther context by saying that the assumption that the Samaritan woman "has treated marriage flippantly in the past . . . clashes with the other details John gives. He presents her as an inquisitive religious seeker who is trusted—perhaps even admired—by her fellow townspeople."[12]

The Gospel writer does not give us a reason why she had five husbands, but Cohick reminds us, "Exploring first-century reali-ties helps us imagine how her life might have unfolded."[13] Professor Cohick also provides plausible reasons for her marital status based on the culture of the Ancient Near East. She writes:

> It is more likely that her five marriages and current arrangement were the results of unfortunate events that took the lives of several of her husbands. Perhaps one or two of them divorced her, or maybe she initiated divorce in one case. As for her current situation, perhaps she had no dowry and thus no formal marriage, meaning her status was similar to a concubine's. Perhaps the man she was currently with was old and needed care, but his children didn't want to share their inheritance with her, so he gave her no dowry docu-ment. Perhaps he was already married, making her his second wife. While the ancient Jewish culture allowed it, such an arrangement

went against Jesus's definition of marriage (Matt. 19:4–6). It makes sense, then, that Jesus would say she wasn't married.[14]

It also makes sense that we just took the time to break this down. Like not skipping the Scriptures that include long generational lists, not skipping this important background helps ground us in biblical times and God's Word.

What we discover is that instead of projecting untoward motives and character onto the woman, we must consider that she was caught in a web of relationships dictated by the patriarchal culture of which she was a part for her survival.

When pressed by Jesus, she spoke the truth about her situation. That's it. Nothing more. Nothing less. Jesus did not come to judge her, call her names, or shame her. He asked a question about her circumstances within a patriarchal system to which she responded truthfully. She shifted the conversation when she responded to Jesus's insight into her life. That is the power of the woman's declaration about her marital status. It was the truth she shared that moved the conversation deeper.

Sister leaders, we do that as Black women. We can speak the truth that moves relationships, systems, and organizations. It's that truth that sets us and others free. We now must tell the truth that the patriarchal forces that have interpreted the woman of Samaria in biased terms are the same forces that attempt to tarnish our leadership as Black women.

Defying the Bias

Critically rereading the woman of Samaria's story gives us insight into defying bias. First and foremost, those who study the woman of Samaria must recognize the bias in the literature about her. It's important to demystify it and establish tactics to defy and confront it. To defy bias as Black women leaders is to challenge it and not let it block us from our purpose in leading businesses, developing staff members, challenging and changing organizational policies, and cultivating productive and empowering places of work and worship.

Even though it may be difficult to admit, bias is real and occurs at *every* leadership level—from the first-line supervisor to the executive in the boardroom. Women pastors leading congregations face gender bias, as do executive directors of nonprofit agencies. Chances are, wherever you are in your leadership journey, you have faced some form of prejudice, are facing it now, or will face it in the future. For Black women, it's the intersection of gender and racial bias that is particularly troubling, and striving to overcome, navigate around, or overwork to disprove these biases can have harmful effects on our overall wellbeing.

Recognize Bias and Potential Barriers

Several years ago, during a session for executive women, a woman stated, "A few of us in our department shared our prework with some of the younger women in the office, and they were adamant they don't face these biases anymore." Before I could respond, other women clamored, "Oh, just let them stay here long enough; they'll experience it." We unpacked this notion of the prevalence of gender bias, especially at pivotal career junctures. We concluded that bias is so much a part of the system that some women don't see it; they assume it is just the way things are. If company leaders didn't make changes, these younger women might experience bias at critical points in their careers, even if they didn't realize it.

Two areas where these biases often have an effect are during promotion considerations and in meetings. At promotions, Black women are more likely to have to prove they are ready for promotions, while men are assumed to be prepared. In meetings, male executives reveal their bias in the frequency and types of questions they ask of their Black women executive colleagues. Black women leaders at every level have to prove we've earned the right to sit at the table. It can get exhausting!

We must recognize the distinct ways bias stemming from a racialized patriarchal narrative shows up for us. Remember, sexism and racism are not so blatant anymore. People have become very skilled in masking their prejudices even from themselves. For Black women leaders, patriarchy manifests in the form of gendered racism, which "is defined as the distinct form of oppression manifested in stereotypes of Black and African American women as being angry, emasculatingly independent, and/or hypersexualized."[15] Below we will unpack four stereotypes that are often applied to Black women.

The Oversexualization of Black Women

As Black women, we live at the nexus or intersection of race and gender. This intersectionality includes our spirituality, sexuality, and social class. But our sexuality has been relegated to stereotypic patterns of oversexualization. The most common label for oversexualizing Black women is the Jezebel trope.

The roots of the Jezebel stereotype run deep. Historically, to justify the rape and sexual assault of Black women, white supremacists created the trope of the sexually promiscuous Black woman called a Jezebel. Jezebel was the queen and wife of King Ahab in the Hebrew Bible. She defied the religious orthodoxy of her husband's culture. "Over time, the label Jezebel came to signify a woman who is sexually promiscuous, untrustworthy, and a threat to society. In the American context, the Jezebel stereotype was weaponized against enslaved Black women."[16]

Today we can see use of the Jezebel trope extended beyond sexuality to include the outspoken outsider woman who breaks the norms of the established male hierarchy and asserts her agency and power. It can manifest as a barrier or bias for Black women leaders when others attempt to minimize our successes by accusing us of sleeping our way to the top or using our personalities to manipulate our way into jobs we aren't qualified for. Worrying about these potential complaints can make us hypervigilant in our workplace interactions. As one unmarried executive woman recounted, she had to be careful whom she brought with her to after-hours workplace functions lest she be labeled as promiscuous.

The systemic effects of this oversexualizing result in Black women disproportionately experiencing workplace sexual harassment.[17] The implication is that Black women are innately sexually promiscuous and, therefore, open to inappropriate sexual advances. This pattern has to be acknowledged and addressed *and* reported. And organizational leaders must believe and protect Black women from retaliation when they report such harassment.

Additionally, we must not internalize such bias. Doing so will increase the likelihood that we will solely see our flaws and not our attributes. Recently, I met with a Black Christian woman who struggled with esteem issues that stemmed from workplace bias. The well within prompted me to ask her, "Tell me five things you like about yourself." She struggled. Big time. It took quite a while, but she finally had five affirmations to hold on to for future use.

Can *you* list five things about yourself that you like? Try not to move on until you name—and claim—them. Write them down in a journal, in a note-keeping app, or on a sticky note where you will see the list often.

The Invisibility of Black Women

A few years back, I visited a church that was the host venue for a service of an international religious organization. When it was time for the host pastor to give remarks, he said something I'll never forget. In commending the national leaders of this organization, he said, "Ours is one of the largest religious organizations led by Black men."

Now, mind you, dedicated Black men *and* women comprised this religious organization. Women held leadership positions, though the organization's culture privileged male leadership, in that the senior most ecclesiastical leadership positions were allowed to be held only by men. This pastor's statement, in effect, rendered the women in ancillary leadership positions invisible.

Yes, many of us are a part of churches formed in resistance to white supremacy, and we as a people are quick to call out racism. But we must be just as quick to call out sexism and not push women into the shadows where they are neither seen nor heard.

As an example of workplace invisibility, Ashley, an executive director, shared how she sometimes recognized when stakeholders of other races ignored her in meetings. She said, "They talk to everyone else at the table but me, and that's ok. I'm going to let them do that until I get ready to talk." When she was ready to assert her voice, she said she let everyone in the meeting know, "I've been patient. You've had a whole conversation without me, and now I want you to hear my perspective." When the invisibility bias is operating, we've got to insert ourselves into the process—and take up our space—so others can see and hear us and never forget why we are at the table to begin with.

The Second-String Leadership Team

Back when I taught at a local university, one afternoon the administrative assistant in another department came running into my office to share what she saw as exciting news. She had been listening to a popular Christian radio teacher she'd found insightful. She named him and exclaimed that she'd been struck by his remark that, "God has no choice but to call women to lead when men are not in their rightful places." I immediately responded, "That suggests God has placed women on God's second-string team because of our gender." In other words, that line of thinking is like God telling us, "Suit up, women, and be ready to play while the first-string team of men leads the way. If I put you in the game, it will be because men couldn't lead." That's an insult to both us as Black women and to the men around us.

More recently, my husband came home and mentioned he'd heard a message on a Christian radio station he thought I'd find troubling. It turns out it was the same Bible teacher, some *twenty* years later, espousing the same point. Embedded in this message was the assumption that God has a hierarchy of leadership based on gender. Sisters, please know that God calls based on God's sovereign purposes and will call whomever God chooses to call.

As leaders, we are not an afterthought of God predicated on whether men step up to lead. God calls women to lead in ministry or the marketplace because that is what we were created to do. God has no gendered second-string team—we *all* are essential to God's plan.

Women also experience this second-string bias when company decision-makers assume we are a better fit for support or hospitality roles instead of operational roles responsible for a company's profit and loss or outward-facing roles like sales. Too often, Black women are career pathed into human resources; diversity, equity, and incusion; and communication roles and not given the requisite opportunities and experiences to lead in operations or sales. If care and support are part of our skill sets or desired experiences, we should enthusiastically go for those positions. They are just as important within a company. But we should have the choice and not be shoved into a support role because of gender bias.

The Angry Black Woman

The Angry Black Woman narrative is a pervasive stereotype that talented Black women leaders face. The common narrative is "deeply rooted in American culture and dates back to chattel slavery in the US."[18]

This narrative assumes we always have a bad attitude and are forever angry. The way the trope goes, Black women are angry when we

- do not gossip or are "too quiet" (a constant complaint).
- do not echo prevailing views or dare to offer a different perspective or opinion.

- defend ourselves.
- do not laugh at racist or misogynistic jokes.
- refuse to be scapegoats for others' mistakes.
- are not easily manipulated.

That's the short list of why people throw the Angry Black Woman label our way. Sisters—as we know—there is not that much anger in the world! Yet we are labeled as angry anyway.

The effect of such labeling hinders our wellbeing in a very specific way because it taps into our emotions and causes us to second-guess ourselves. The threat of the label can trap us, and feeling trapped always brings out a host of emotions, including the very anger we try so hard to manage. Let's face it: the exclusion, gaslighting, and pressure to assimilate in organizational life can bring up a host of emotions in us.

And honestly, we have as much of a right as other people to experience and express our emotions, including anger. But we must not internalize the narrative that we are all Angry Black Women. Following Dr. Chanequa Walker-Barnes in her literary scrunching of StrongBlackWoman[19] to differentiate between the stereotype and a Black woman who is strong, we must know being angry as a Black woman does not make us an AngryBlackWoman (or ABW). It makes us human—a human created in the image of God, who likewise expressed anger.

Emotions are part of the human makeup. Yet Black women's emotions are pejorative, while white men's shouting, frustration, and anger in the workplace, for instance, are seen as passionate leadership.

For some leaders, it's easier and more commonplace to label a Black woman who speaks up against being unfairly treated, who voices concern over a process, or who responds to an offense with the stereotypic ABW label than to look critically at the system the woman is challenging—or even to look more critically at themselves and their own prejudices. Like the woman of Samaria, her five previous husbands and current man weren't really the issue for Jesus. No. Jesus came to free her from a system that produced conditions in which she had to have five husbands and a sixth man to survive.

For our souls' sakes, the next time any of us are confronted with the AngryBlackWoman label or hear of another Black woman labeled as such, we must consider if the person using the tired, inappropriate label is deflecting from taking a serious look at the issues we raised. We may even say, "Seriously, is that the best you've got?" (Ok, we may not say it out loud, but I'm sure we'll be thinking it.)

Tell the Truth

These are just four systemic biases Black women leaders face. When we are confronted with these caricatures, we must tell the truth about the barriers and biases we face individually and collectively. Such truth-telling about marriage and divorce in patriarchal cultures enables us to recognize the narrative bias commentators, mainly from the Western tradition, have used to misinterpret the story of the woman of Samaria.

Worse, this narrative bias has obscured the strength this woman brought to the encounter. It minimizes her role in the Gospel story, rendering her invisible as a disciple and labeling her a problematic woman in her questioning of Jesus. Similar biases render Black women invisible, secondary, and as threats to organizations if we let them. Instead, we need to speak up and tell the truth.

My truth-telling about issues facing Black women in leadership started years ago as I was consulting with multinational corporations on their women's leadership development programs. Within the programs, I noticed a pattern that there were always just a few Black women in attendance, and I wondered why there were not more Black women advancing to high levels within these companies. And worse, how had no one other than me noticed? I committed then to broadening my reach and calling this out to the companies that hired me.

We must name the reality that for the longest time women's advancement in organizational spaces meant *white* women's advancement. The truth is that, even when companies sought gender diversity, the underlying biases meant that the default category for women in diversity programs was white women. So I committed to developing additional programs and content that specifically tapped into the needs of Black women.

We must tell the truth that even from the beginning of the women's movement, Black women's issues were deemed invisible and nonessential to white women. Our issues or experiences are distinct. Now, we welcome allies to join us in our work of leading well as Black women, but we need partners to see, hear, and heed our wisdom.

Remember Who We Are

One of the most critical elements of defying racialized gender bias is remembering who we are. In chapter 2, we affirmed who we are as Black women loved and called by God. The affirmation of our identity in Christ must be an ongoing practice. As women created in God's image, loved by God, called by Christ, and filled with the Spirit, we represent the Lord wherever we are. *Who* we are has a bearing on *how* we defy bias.

Managing the tension of calling out the bias while letting our light shine can be one of the most challenging things to do. So let me say this: it is a both/and proposition, not either/or. We have to call out and address the bias and remind ourselves that doing so is part of letting our lights shine. Shining a light on bias is part of our call, for the light shines and exposes darkness. The darkness of bias "can never extinguish" our lights (John 1:5).

Sisters, remember that in order to keep our lights shining, we have got to spend time at the well!

I remember a consulting assignment not too long ago in which I was providing strategic direction for a company-wide DEI initiative. I worked closely with the executive team, and we were making great strides in the slow, methodic work of corporate culture change.

In one meeting, I mentioned that the leaders were going to need to embed DEI principles into all their core people processes and operating systems. An executive bellowed (yes, bellowed), "You mean we are going to have to walk on eggshells all the time?" Immediately I asked, rather straightforwardly, "What do you mean by walking on eggshells?" He again yelled, "Don't interrupt me. I wasn't finished." Granted, this executive came from a culture different from mine, and there may be culturally diverse approaches to handling conflict. Still, no amount of cultural differences would justify this man yelling at me.

I, however, prayerfully invoked what my Granny called shut-mouth grace. I clamped my mouth shut, being mindful of the junior people in the meeting. I also direct-messaged the Chief Human Resources officer, who was also on the call, and typed, "We will need to talk about this at the next executive steering committee meeting, because he will not yell at me ever again."

Sisters, now you already know, don't you? I was shaken inside but had to maintain my posture in that meeting. I had to remember who I was so that man would not forget it.

Name It

Robin, the CEO of a community health institute, cared passionately for her community and led programs to address social aspects of health for people in her community. The institute launched after-school programs for local children and developed programs that helped community members with housing issues, employment, and overall wellness. Robin adeptly called out racism in meetings when it happened. She didn't wait; she didn't go behind closed doors to talk about it. She named it.

For instance, in one meeting, the leaders of a consulting group came to secure business from the institute. The group was not racially diverse, and no one in the group looked like Robin's team or the community her agency served. Their proposal showed a lack of understanding of the community, and Robin called it out.

She said, "You want to come into this community riding your horse to save the people, and you don't even know what they need. That is not going to be received well in our community." She continued, "We need people at the table who look like the people you want to serve. If you want to understand the culture and you want people to talk to you about what their real issues are, you've got to build trust with the people in the community."

Implicit in their approach was the bias that they knew what was best for that community. However, they had no connection to the people or understanding of their values and needs. Robin would have none of it and called it like she saw it: a white savior bias.

When we feel like there is an injustice, we have to name it. As leaders, we must make the implicit explicit; we address the issue and do not let the biases fester like a sore, spreading and infecting the culture or our personal wellbeing.

Confront with Curiosity

For years, many of us have coached people to assume positive intent when confronted with bias. You know what I mean. A colleague or another leader says something that doesn't sit well and smacks of bias. We're encouraged to assume the colleague had positive intentions—a tactic intended to give the colleague the benefit of the doubt.

Recently my cousin Dr. Heather Sanders, who leads an organizational consulting practice, asked a thought-provoking question. "In those situations when someone says something offensive, why would we assume anything? We really can't know someone else's intent." Instead, Heather advises people to remain curious about the comment or action and ask questions about what the person meant or intended.

We might use questions such as, "What did you mean by that?" or "Can you help me understand what you are saying?" Each of us needs to mentally prepare a set of questions such as these that we can use to confront a microaggression or offensive action. This way, we navigate the situation to hear and understand the person's intent. From there, we can turn the situation into a teachable moment and discuss with the person the impact of their words or actions on us. If the person is open, this process allows them to examine their biased statement or action.

Prioritize Impact over Intent

When faced with a biased comment or action by another person, especially in leadership, we must recognize a gap between what the person may have intended and the impact of their statement or action on us. And we must prioritize addressing the impact of words or deeds on ourselves and others when it comes to bias. We have to be clear about the effects or implications of misplaced words or deeds in order to see change.

For example, many women in my leadership programs have expressed concern over being labeled as aggressive. I coach them to address the aggressive stereotype by distinguishing between aggressiveness and assertiveness. There is a difference.

Aggressive people force their way and opinion upon others. They are only concerned about their own voice or power. Assertive people have respect for their own voice or power as well as the voices of others. They will assert their opinion or actions without disrespecting another person. Assertive Black women get unfairly labeled as aggressive, though our words and actions have not indicated disrespect for another person.

In those times when a colleague labels a woman as aggressive, whether the person intended it as an insult or to be hurtful or not, we must share the impact of using that worn-out, unwarranted stereotype. Continued use of it perpetuates an age-old bias detrimental to Black women. The effect of such labels is to stigmatize outspoken women and diminish the confidence of otherwise confident women.

Draw Strength from Our Community of Allies

After the meeting in which the executive yelled at me, I called my friend and executive DEI leader Tyronne Stoudemire. I vented and released. He listened and empathized. I drew strength from that conversation. From there, I went to the well, spent time in prayer, and asked God for a strategy to deal with this client. And sure enough, the Holy Spirit gave me the plan to hold a difficult conversation with that executive leader.

Sisters, we have got to pray for the courage to have these difficult conversations. In calling him, I demonstrated leadership that demanded respect and broke through an interpersonal barrier that could have prevented the two of us from moving forward together. All too often, if we want respect, we have to show people how to respect us. Ask the Spirit for the courage to do so!

Most senior and executive leaders will tell you that as they advanced in leadership, they grew in confidence and shored up their reputation and brand to such an extent that allies readily joined in defending their ideas and projects.

As we advance in our leadership journey, we have to build our network and our supportive community. Our community of allies helps us in leading well. We can draw strength from our community of Black women, other women, and men allies. If we know we will be dealing with a difficult person who has exhibited bias in the past, for example, we can check in with one of our allies and develop strategies for dealing with this person.

Create Healing Spaces

When Jesus came to Sychar, the Samaritan village where he met this woman, he stopped at Jacob's well to rest while the disciples went into the village to get food. The well was a community well—a gathering place for the people. It turns out this community well also became a spiritually healing space for this woman and her neighbors as they came to meet the Messiah.

To defy bias, we need to get to or create healing spaces for our community.

Many churches and Christian women's conferences have often been that space of healing from the psychic and emotional stress of leading while Black and woman. Those healing spaces just don't happen in church or women's conferences, though. In the early days of doing this work, I had one client for which I led a unique program for women at the most senior levels of leadership in their organization. We piloted this program in four cities and limited the invitations to twenty-five women at the senior vice president level.

For each session, I started the day by setting the day's expectations. They were there to listen to and support each other. I was there to provide models and tools to help them lead and advance to the next level or to get their voices heard more powerfully in their current roles. Together we were there to support and listen to each other. We were not there to do male-bashing, gripe, or complain. (Too often, some people think male-bashing is on the agenda simply because we do not accept patriarchal mindsets. Not so!)

Our goal was to walk away with more insight and more strategies for success. Most of all, I reminded them that we were there to have some fun enjoying the learning journey and each other. Yes, we can have fun defying bias and enjoy the healing process.

We created something so special that, for me, the feeling lingered in the air after the participants had left. I experienced that as an anointing; the Holy Spirit had shown up in our moments of learning and truth-telling. I sensed a weight had been lifted off many of those women as each realized they were not imagining things when it came to gender and racial bias, they were not crazy, and they were not in this battle by themselves.

And most empowering, they walked away with options.

That is the power of leading as a Christian woman in the marketplace. Healing and wholeness can take place wherever the Spirit of the Lord is! Of course, the Spirit of the Lord goes with us wherever we go. But when we spend time at the well, we are more sensitive to the Spirit's leading.

Lift as We Climb

Bias shows up in decisions, comments, and actions of people with whom we are in a relationship: coworkers, colleagues, other leaders, managers, and direct reports. Yet as leaders we exist within a system, a structure. As we navigate the gendered racism in the systems we lead, we begin to develop processes and approaches that can eliminate or at least mitigate structural biases against other Black women and everyone else too.

As leaders, we must ask about and address bias in the talent acquisition and recruiting processes. That's why some of us are called to these roles to ensure equitable access for women and men who look like us to spaces not designed for us. Organizational leaders must address policies and practices in making job assignments, cultivating an inclusive culture, and assuring equity in the advancement of all talent, especially for Black women who have long been left out of the senior and executive roles.

Connie Lindsey advanced to the executive vice president ranks as the first Black woman in the investment bank where she worked. A leader in the community ardently committed to our culture, Connie passionately believed in the Black women's club movement motto: "Lift as we climb."

And she did just that. She created a structure to help other women advance. She championed the development of women's comentoring circles in her firm to identify, develop, and promote other women leaders. These circles were diverse in ethnicity, experience, and profession and were instrumental in getting women into the leadership pipeline at that bank. The circles have evolved but remain a vital part of the structure.

Lifting as we climb will also entail modeling practices that invite teams and mentees to pursue self-care. How many of us don't take sick days and keep working until we literally drop? Rather than making us look like superwomen, this actually signals to those around us that they should do the same. Let's do better so that other Black women will be empowered to take care of themselves *before* they get into leadership or while they are holding down roles. Again, leading well is a wholistic approach. We must bring our whole selves to our leadership positions—or leave those selves at home if we are ill. It's better to be at home than in the hospital—or worse!

Wherever we are, as we identify structural and systemic bias, we can work with other leaders within the system to address the bias in it.

Sister leaders, leading well entails being honest about the relationships we hold in the systems we lead and about the interpersonal bias and inherent bias we face in those systems and structures. We can't ignore them, and we won't let them stop us.

LEADING WELL REFLECTION QUESTIONS

1. As you reflect on your leadership, which of the common biases reviewed in this chapter have you experienced the most? How have you addressed them? Looking back on these experiences, what might you do differently now because of reading and/or discussing this chapter?

2. Which strategies for defying bias listed in this chapter resonated with you? How might you use them in your leadership?

LEADING WELL PRACTICE: JOURNALING

In your journal, reflect on the effects of the leadership system you are in. Do you find yourself defensive because of patriarchal game-playing? Do you get angry at comments or actions that hinder you or other women, yet don't express your concerns for fear of being labeled an Angry Black Woman?

Tell the truth about your situation. Review the tactics offered in this chapter and develop your strategy for defying bias as part of your leading well journey.

FIVE

PERCEIVE YOUR POSSIBILITIES

> I perceive that You are a prophet.
> John 4:19 NKJV

Though the Holy Spirit is ever with us, there are times when we become more acutely aware of the Spirit's working in our lives. The Spirit prods us to see that it's time for a change, time for whatever might be next for each of us.

In those times in our leadership, the Spirit brings us fresh insight. We know in these moments of truth that there is more for us than what we are experiencing at present. In these moments of awakening, we must recognize there are more possibilities than we could imagine on our own.

Prophetic Moments

When Jesus revealed what he knew about the Samaritan woman, she recognized the prophetic moment she was in with this man who became less of a stranger the more she talked with him. Awakened and alerted that this stranger knew about her life, she recognized this knowledge wasn't just about her but was also about him. "Stunned by Jesus's extraordinary knowledge of her life, the woman [could] now see him with new eyes."[1] Her new eyes led to a new perspective and possibilities for witnessing and leadership. Likewise, with new eyes we can see the opportunities of all that God has for us.

The Samaritan woman acknowledged Jesus as a prophet. From there, she ushered them both into a prophetic conversation about worship, and in so doing lived into a prophetic moment that ultimately led to the revelation of this stranger's true identity.

Throughout his Gospel, John uses a series of self-declarations or "I Am" statements to show how Jesus revealed himself to the people he encountered (John 6:35; 8:12; 10:7, 11, 14; 11:25; 14:6; 15:1). The first "I Am" statement in John is shared with this woman as Jesus reveals, "I AM the Messiah!" (4:26).

I can't help but think his unveiling also disclosed something to her about herself. She was a worthy conversation partner. She received revelation that no doubt connected in her soul and moved her, as we will see later, to leave her water jar of tradition and follow the plethora of possibilities now burning in her heart.

Isn't that true for us as well? Sometimes barriers within ourselves hinder us from moving forward into leadership or to the next level. The internal barrier may be a lack of confidence or it may be fear. As we grow in our faith and seek the Spirit, the Lord can help us break through any barriers of doubt, fear, or insecurity.

Seeking the God of Possibilities

As their conversation moved to worship, the Samaritan woman asked Jesus "what was at the time the most pressing theological question separating Jews and Samaritans: Is God to be worshiped in Jerusalem . . . or on the Samaritan mountain of Gerizim (v. 20)?"[2]

According to Samaritan theology, the Messiah would not be a descendant of David (as Jewish culture of the time proclaimed) but a prophet like Moses (as promised in Deut. 18:18–19). The Samaritans hoped the Messiah would reveal all things upon his return and restore true worship in the northern kingdom. In other words, "the woman is pursuing a careful investigation of the identity of Jesus who has already indicated his affinity with the patriarchs and his prophetic capacity to 'tell her all things.'"[3] It turns out that both were true: Jesus was a prophet like Moses and also a descendant of David.

Jesus revealed the connection between the living water and authentic worship in this prophetic moment. "The indwelling Spirit is the internal well of living water 'springing up to life eternal' (4:14). The Spirit is also the inspiration and source of true worship."[4] This gift of the Spirit that "issues in divine worship"[5] is not "bound to any location and enables believers to worship God properly 'in spirit and truth.'"[6]

We have seen a certain quality of the Samaritan woman emerge repeatedly. She asked questions that were "risky, courageous, and deeply theological."[7] We, too, can courageously and boldly ask the Lord questions about anything, but especially as they have a bearing on our leadership. The Samaritan woman was deeply steeped in her culture and used that cultural knowledge to query Jesus and recognize him for who he indeed was.

The Possibility to Change

Through the living water within, we can address complex issues and challenges for those we lead and for ourselves. As Black women leaders of faith, we must stay abreast of issues affecting other Black women, especially those we lead. And as leaders, whether we are in ministry or the marketplace, we must be ready, prepared, and prayerful enough to ask tough questions and open enough to hear what the Spirit is saying.

Through coaching and self-reflection, one woman who led in the marketplace in a very old-school, white male–dominated industry became very adept at asking questions that led to the revelation of new leadership possibilities. I'll call her Evelyn. She had adopted a very stern leadership style to reinforce that she was *the* leader of her team. This style differed from the one she exhibited at church, home, and even with her close work friends. I sense she never felt safe enough to be her fully authentic self in her leadership role in her company. That is not unusual.

The style Evelyn had adopted was a power-over approach to leading. She had read about the teachings of early twentieth-century management consultant Mary Parker Follett.[8] Feminist scholars dub Follett the "prophet of management" because she wrote and taught participative or collaborative leadership principles and practices well before more prominent men did so.[9]

According to Parker Follett, *power-over* is a coercive "power of some person or group over some other person or group." By contrast, *power-with* is a "jointly developed power" or a "power of interactive influence."[10]

Most of us don't wake up each day thinking we will bully others or contemplate how to wield power over them. But leading from a power-over style begins to happen subtly and can occur when we don't assess the underlying motivation or reasons we lead the way we do. In other words, when we don't examine the heart of our leadership, we can show up in ways that are antithetical to our wellbeing and that of others.

Sometimes a power-over approach to leading occurs because demands stretch us, and it seems more manageable to tell, command, or bark out orders. Deadlines are pressing. Requests are piling up. So we flex our ideas over the ideas of the team. We don't take time to listen. We impose our methods onto the team or department solely because we know these methods have worked for us, and we think to ourselves, *If they just do it my way, I know it can be successful.* This is a very hierarchical style, akin to patriarchal leadership.

This subtle power-over mindset can occur in other leadership contexts, not just at work. The teacher who takes delight in marking student papers with red ink or font. The caregiver who is unduly impatient with their loved one and does not give them the options of choices they can still make. The parent who is unduly authoritarian with their child, thus dimming the child's light of creativity and confidence.

Leading in overpowering ways violates the choices of others to express their God-given agency, creativity, and ability to adapt and adopt new approaches within the prescribed limits of the group, team, or department.

In contrast, leaders who lead from a place of possibilities and honor their own and their team members' wellbeing develop more of a power-with approach to leading. These leaders stay open to the Spirit, hearing and heeding the insight, wisdom, and direction that flow from the living water.

Back to Evelyn. The unintentional outcomes of using that overpowering style for her team resulted in high turnover, relational distance from her team members, and poor performance. She realized what she was doing in a moment of truth—her prophetic moment—and asked herself why she led the way she did. It was not healthy or helpful for her or those she led. As she did the inner work, she realized she led that way out of her insecurities and fear of being vulnerable and authentic with the people at work.

Evelyn shifted her leadership style from power-over to power-with. She adjusted her mindset from *I am right, and my team members are not going to get one over on me* to an influence mindset of *The members of my team are subject matter experts; they have gifts and skills, and together we can perform well and meet our goals.*

She backed off her overpowering words and deeds and adopted more of a collaborative coaching style. And shortly she reported that she began seeing unprecedented changes in her team. They began to work better with each other and with her and to develop better relationships with other departments, thus providing a better overall customer experience. Team members also began to step up more to take on leadership roles on the team, such as running meetings in Evelyn's absence.

. . . . .

Remember, we lead from who we are, and if what we do as leaders is not aligned with our true selves, we will experience stress related to soul-role misalignment. This occurs when our role does not align with our soul. When the position requires more than the soul is willing to pay, it's time for a soul-role realignment—an intentional reflection on our core values, beliefs, and purpose.

As this soul-role realignment began to happen for Evelyn, she described the changes she made when she shifted from leading to get somewhere, such as the next promotion, to leading from a place of purpose and values that included supporting others to be their best and succeed. In addition to these visible changes with and in her team, she reported a transformational internal shift. Evelyn broke through her harsh internal barrier and began to experience joy in leading.

Yes, soul-felt joy is possible when we lead from a place of wholeness and authenticity and in service to our overall wellbeing and that of our teams, organizations, and institutions. Leading well is about all of this. Sisters, I want all of us to imagine now the possibilities of our leadership that can result in each of us experiencing or recapturing joy.

Too often, we, as Black women, have had to fit ourselves into a leadership box of expectations from our organizations, institutions, churches, and schools. These boxes don't always serve us well. They can constrain us. Sometimes they minimize or ignore the differences, distinct perspectives, and experiences we bring. People who did not look like us and did not have us in mind founded and maintained these organizations and institutions. The resulting organizational cultures express values that minimize or sometimes are in direct conflict with the values we bring from our culture and faith.

Leadership coaches can serve as the conduits for those prophetic moments in which we gain insight into why we do what we do and help us hear, envision, and see what is possible. But there's more. Leading from the well of the Holy Spirit keeps our hearts open to what God is doing in us, around us, and for us. As Scripture teaches, "'No eye has seen, no ear has heard, and no mind has imagined what God has prepared for those who love [God].' But it was to us that God revealed these things by [God's] Spirit. For [God's] Spirit searches out everything and shows us God's deep secrets" (1 Cor. 2:9–10).

In Spirit and in Truth

The Holy Spirit will reveal what is possible and what has already been planned for us by God! Sister leaders, as part of our wellness routines, we must develop a regular, intimate time with God, a regular time of going to the well of living water. Through the Spirit, we access the spiritual realm (Eph. 2:18), and from the Spirit of truth, we receive revelation and insight that shore up our leadership and life.

Worship is accessing or entering God's presence through the Holy Spirit. A broad, all-encompassing term, *worship* includes prayer, singing, giving adoration to God, and even, as we saw in chapter 3, deep breathing in the presence of our God. Too often in our contemporary culture, some have reduced worship to a musical genre. Yet worship is so much more than any sort of music, and it is critical to the life and leadership of anyone who will lead, especially Black Christian women.

When we spend time with God in God's presence, we bask in God's love. Through worship, we ascribe to God qualities and characteristics due to God because God is worthy. A time of intimacy with God, worship is healing and transformative, the vehicle that brings us into God's presence, and in the presence of the Lord there "is fullness of joy" (Ps. 16:11 NKJV). I once heard someone put it this way: "Praise gets us in the door; worship gets us in the Lord's presence."

Spending time in God's presence opens our hearts before God. God sees us at the deepest level, loves us, and affirms us as children of God. In these times, we hear the heart of God. We access the living water through worship, drinking in its refreshing, healing flow. Through worship, we receive revelation as we enter God's presence and have been given access to God through the Spirit.

It really is a profoundly intimate time. Music can help get us there. Words of adoration can also help get us there, taking our minds off ourselves and things in our lives and pointing our inner consciousness toward God. Walking in nature, God's handiwork, can move us to awe and wonder. Worship can make us vulnerable before God and ultimately gives us the capacity to be open and honest before people.

Worship is a spiritual practice that is both individual and collective, personal and public. We have the privilege of worshiping privately through prayer, in private time with God, and in community with other believers. Remember when the world shut down, and most of our churches closed due to the raging COVID-19 virus? We learned that the church is not a building; worship is not limited to a place, just as Jesus promised.

Whether live, in person, virtually, or in private, worship can open our hearts to the heart of God. It can bring us into a place of closeness in the presence of God and bring us to a place of possibilities.

While worship is a spiritual practice, it can also become a mindset, an attitude of reverence toward the One who is truly in charge and invigorates our leadership. Rooted in ancient practices, many of our contemporary worship practices came out of a worldview of seeing ourselves and all of humanity as "divinely linked, related to, and involved with all creation."[11] As Lisa Allen, author of *A Womanist Theology of Worship*, puts it, this worldview "results in holistic relationships and responses that honor, respect, hear, and acknowledge the entire universe as the Creator's handiwork and how one is called to 'be' as part of that."[12]

From our cultural heritage, we know worship was a means for our ancestors to experience "a liberative sense of joy, amid unbearable sorrow."[13] It was a time when our people gathered and were uplifted and strengthened through songs, prayers, and liberating preaching. In worship, they experienced cathartic breakthroughs expressed in raised hands, stomping feet, tapping toes, running, jumping, ecstatic utterances, speaking in tongues, moaning, weeping, and holding each other. We hail from a people who broke through the worst existential burdens through anointed worship.

The same is true for us today. Our worship services are places in which we gather and receive solace, comfort, strength, and healing. Gathering in our faith communities enables us to let our guards down in the presence of the Lord and fellow believers and receive strength for our ongoing leadership journeys.

We can't separate or bifurcate our being into segments, allowing parts of us to show up in different contexts. At work, we are leaders; at home, a parent; at church, a volunteer. Yes, those are all different roles, but to be authentic, our core identity, who we are inside, must inform every role.

Yes, we learn to code-switch and adapt our behavior in authentic ways to our varied contexts—that's being a smart leader who understands her audience. But we can't try to change our identity to fit into someone else's expectations—that's assimilation, and it is unhealthy.

What worship does is bring us into God's presence, opening our hearts to what the Spirit wants to reveal to us. From that place, we live to express the truth of who we are to others.

Receive the Revelation from the Spirit

You see, once the Samaritan woman shifted the conversation to worship, she ushered herself and Jesus into a theological dialogue. But it was also a conversation about power: the tension between these two cultures centered on the place of worship. Or, put another way, the divide between them centered on who had the power to determine the proper place of worship. The Samaritans looked for the Messiah to establish the northern kingdom as the site of worship for everyone. The Jewish people of the time held firmly to the power to decree that the only legitimate place of worship was the temple in Jerusalem. Both were power-over moves, with each culture believing its way was the right way.

Jesus came on the scene, busted the power-over moves, and expanded the notion of worship to wherever, whenever—as long as it is done in Spirit and truth. Again, "The spirit [God] gives is not bound to any location and enables believers to worship God properly, 'in spirit and truth.'"[14]

Worship thus conceived becomes a power-with move in which all believers recognize the true power is with God, and God is seeking people who are willing vessels to empower with and through the Spirit.

Worship thus conceived relieves us of our status as little gods who wield power over others and, instead, sensitizes our hearts to the power of God and helps us lead in ways that empower others and enhance our wellbeing.

How Worship Opens Possibilities

So much of leadership is about vision and possibilities. But sometimes our understanding of what is possible is limited by our interior barriers. On numerous occasions, Jesus taught his followers that possibilities lie in the realm of faith, saying, for example, "Anything is possible if a person believes" (Mark 9:23) and "What is impossible for people is possible with God" (Luke 18:27).

Worship, in the broadest sense, aligns us with the will of God. Our personal and collective worship enhance our ability to lead relationally, discern strategy, and become open to being vulnerable.

To be vulnerable is to show our weaknesses. We all have them. Yet many of us fear vulnerability lest others exploit those weaknesses and harm us. For StrongBlackWomen, shame is the cost of being vulnerable. When we show emotional or mental/cognitive weakness, we feel we shouldn't have those weaknesses. We've received messages throughout our lives that we are supposed to be strong even if we don't feel it. So we try to fake it until we make it; we mask up, suit up, armor up.

But the soul is funny: our masquerade does not fool it. It hurts when it hurts. When it's overloaded, it short-circuits. When wounded, it cries out and sometimes whimpers.

For StrongBlackWomen, showing vulnerability in contexts that diminish our worth is hard to do. I get it. I've been there and done that. We wear a veneer of strength. But most people don't realize how thin the front is.

We need the Spirit, because the Holy Spirit helps us in our weaknesses. When we are so emotionally and spiritually expended that we have no words even to pray, according to Romans 8:26–27, the Spirit prays for us with "groanings that cannot be expressed in words" yet prays "in harmony with God's own will." The Spirit takes our soul's cries to the throne of God, translates them, and then deposits in our hearts the strategy, revelation, and Word needed.

As followers of Christ, we are known by Jesus intimately. Through worship, we, too, can perceive so much more of what the Lord has for us. Worship can provide clarity.

Visionary Black women perceive that what's impossible to some is possible through God. Leadership so often is an act of faith, of spiritual perception. A great deal of leadership is casting a vision to get people to move toward what can be. Leadership is instilling hope in people who are in hopeless situations.

We hail from a legacy of Black women of faith who perceived possibilities for themselves, their communities, their nation, and their world. Harriet Tubman perceived traveling to freedom when the institution of slavery stripped Black people of liberty. Mary McLeod Bethune perceived education for Black people when legal barriers prevented Black children from getting access to quality education. Ida B. Wells perceived the ending of legalized lynching of Black people. Shirley Chisolm perceived the possibility of electing a Black woman as president of the United States.

More recently, Stacey Abrams perceived voter equity for Black people and, through her grassroots organizing in 2020, registered over 880,000 new voters in Georgia to combat the voter suppression that had occurred when she first ran for governor.[15] Kamala Harris perceived herself as shattering the glass ceiling to become the first Black and South Asian woman elected vice president of the United States. In her acceptance speech the night of her victory, she gave tribute to the women who "paved the way for this moment tonight," especially "the Black women who are too often overlooked, but so often prove they are the backbone of our democracy."[16] Vice President Harris wanted to prove to all children watching that America "is a country of possibilities," as she declared, "I may be the first woman to hold this office. But I won't be the last."[17]

We must ask, What possibilities are percolating in our spirits, ready to be brought to life? What options are bubbling to the surface of our consciousness?

Accessing the living water through worship will bring these inchoate ideas into formation. Developing the discipline and mindset of worship will help us sense where the Spirit is leading and open our hearts to hear. Through this intimate communion time with God, our souls can be refreshed, our perceptions clarified, and our resolve strengthened to follow the leading of the Spirit.

Perceiving Possibilities for Promotions

Fay received the opportunity to apply for a C-suite role in a large urban school district. When asked to apply, initially she was not going to go for the position as she was quite successful and comfortable in her current role. Yet, here came something new.

We never know when God is about to do a new thing in our leadership and our lives. As the prophet declared to the ancient nation of Israel, and as the Spirit will declare at strategic times in our lives: "See, I am doing a new thing! Now it springs up; do you not perceive it?" (Isa. 43:19 NIV).

So, Fay sought the Lord and talked to her family. Yes, no matter the title or advancement opportunity, leading well entails ensuring the role aligns with the whole of our lives, including our families. It became clear to her that this new role was the direction she was to go in. She recounted, "God began to give me the vision for this role and the system I would lead. Once I received vision, I knew I was on the right track."

Fay went for the promotion and received it. She reports that she and her extensive team are implementing the vision the Lord gave her, and they are experiencing the positive impact of this vision. Sisters, we can perceive possibilities for what God has for us and move forward confidently.

This Samaritan woman's perception of the prophetic turned her dialogue with Jesus into worship. In their exchange, we see worship as a cultural practice and a lifestyle, and ultimately, we can make the connection that worship is how we access the living water and the hopeful possibilities that flow from the Spirit.

LEADING WELL REFLECTION QUESTIONS

1. What does a prophetic moment mean to you? How might the Spirit be beckoning you in this season?

2. In times of transition, we need to be more acutely aware of the possibilities of the next seasons of our lives and leadership. Where are you in terms of transition?

3. What are the things that block your perceptions of possibilities?

4. In chapter 1, I asked you to reimagine what your leadership might become if you genuinely led from the well. Revisit your reflections. As you've learned more about leading well, what shifts in your leadership are you now sensing you need to make?

LEADING WELL PRACTICE: YOUR WORSHIP PLAYLIST

It's popular for social media influencers to share their playlists during specific seasons, such as their summer playlist or their Christmas playlist. Take a moment to compile your worship playlist.

Set aside time for the next few days to spend consistent time in worship listening to the songs on your playlist. Then transition into a prayer of worship, in which you use words of adoration for God. Afterward, spend some time journaling. Note how this time brings you into the presence of God, directs your focus, and opens your heart to what the Lord is saying.

SIX

TRUST OUR WAYS OF KNOWING

I know the Messiah is coming.

John 4:25

My Granny used to say, "You've got to know that you know." That was her way of saying that each of us must be so assured of what we know about ourselves and our experiences that no one can make us doubt the things we have firsthand knowledge about. As a Black church matriarch, Granny primarily referred to salvation when she said this, but I've learned that the need for this knowledge is not limited to the church. Wherever we go, from corporate meetings to boardrooms to community collaborations, we must be ready at a moment's notice to call upon that way of knowing I learned at my Granny's feet.

Knowing for Black Christian women is more than information we amass in our education. Knowing for Black women leaders is a way of navigating new and challenging situations that are often fraught with racist and sexist undercurrents that, if left unaddressed, can threaten to diminish our sense of worth and value and harm our overall wellbeing. It is also about using wisely what we have learned and what we discern for the betterment of ourselves, those around us, and our communities.

The need to call upon this knowing sometimes occurs when we least expect it. But we, as Black women leaders of faith, must be prepared and draw what is needed to handle those challenges from the well of wisdom within each of us. Recently I remembered Granny's lesson when I served as a guest panelist for a Chicago-based consortium that connected new business owners of color with established business owners. The established owners serve as mentors to the new owners in a twelve-month development program.

The mentees of the program were women and men, mainly from the African American community, many of whom were launching a business for the first time. But the executive mentors were predominantly white men plus a few women.

The organizers asked me to focus on providing leadership tips for small business owners. After my copanelist and I introduced ourselves and gave some high-level strategies from each of our respective areas of expertise, the facilitator opened the conversation to the members of the audience to share what, to that point in the program, had resonated with them. It was very affirming to hear participants share their insights from our respective presentations.

All was going smoothly with our exchange of ideas until one man, whom I'll call Mr. Man and whom I quickly realized was one of the mentors, began to coopt the platform to advance his ideas. He first expounded on the need to build a business network, which he had apparently taught the group in a previous session. He then moved on to talk about leadership.

At one point, Mr. Man directed a question toward me, asking if I knew any professors at two elite business schools in Chicago. I wondered where he was going with this line of questioning and how it related to the topic but knew deep inside that it was far from an innocent inquiry. Fortunately, the facilitator voiced what I was thinking.

I know that some people will discount us if we don't have on our résumés what they consider the right school. Quite frankly, some will try to minimize us because, in their estimation, we aren't of the right race and gender.

Not everything I've learned about leadership has been validated or legitimized by business school. In fact, for the audience I was speaking to, my experiences of launching a business as a Black woman and successfully running that business for twenty years connected me to that audience in ways impossible for that older white man. (Always remember, you belong where God places you, regardless of how others may view your résumé!) I had been invited to speak on leadership and, quite frankly, had established a stellar track record of developing and delivering leadership development programs across the world for numerous domestic and multinational companies.

And so I assertively answered his question, letting him know that I had mentored one of the professors of said business school while he was in college and grad school, and we were now colleagues. Then I made a significant pivot.

"Here's what I know," I said, now directing my comments to the intended audience of mentees who wanted my leadership insight. "Depending on where each of you is in your business cycle, you may still be doing a great deal of the heavy lifting. When I started my business, I did everything from developing training programs, editing programs, and marketing my services to keeping the books. You name it. But as you grow, you will go from being an entrepreneur who does everything to a business owner who manages a team of doers, and ultimately you will need to motivate and inspire the people who work for you. That is where leadership comes in. In fact, there are five key points of becoming a leader that small business owners grapple with." I shared those five key points and then invited the audience to go to my website to take my free leadership readiness assessment.

I reestablished the conversation on my terms. By mentioning his connections to key business professors, Mr. Man was demonstrating he could introduce me to these university professionals. He was dangling a carrot—something he could do for me. Yet I knew that this was less about me and more about him establishing his power, and, without even realizing it, he was illustrating his white male privilege with the assumption that he could hijack the presentations of two Black women.

From my perspective, this presentation was not about me; it was not about me becoming connected with his movers and shakers. It was about me serving that audience at that moment with the wisdom I had gained that could help them lead their businesses more wisely.

For generations, Black women have had to read between the lines to know and discern what is really going on in a situation so as not to be duped, discouraged, or destroyed. Years ago, a Black woman sociologist, Dr. Patricia Hill Collins, created a framework that described and honored Black women's ways of knowing. She taught us that our foremothers developed a way of knowing that led to wisdom about life, and noted, "Living life as Black women requires wisdom because knowledge about the dynamics of intersecting oppressions has been essential to US Black women's survival."[1]

Collins also argued that "knowledge without wisdom is adequate for the powerful, but wisdom is essential to the survival of the subordinate."[2] Now, my encounter with Mr. Man was not necessarily a matter of survival. Still, it was a matter of respect and demonstrating to all involved that day that (1) I knew what was really going on there, and (2) I would not allow him to silence my voice or the voice of my colleague.

Outsider Women Know

I think back to the woman at the well and listen to her proclaim to Jesus that "I know the Messiah is coming" (John 4:25). The Greek word from which we translate "know" in this verse, *eidō*, gives the sense of "to see"—but not in the literal sense of seeing with the eyes. Rather it means to see in my Granny's sense of the inner vision of discernment. It can mean "to be aware," "to consider," "to be sure," and "to understand."[3]

This knowing is a way of seeing and recognizing what is happening around us and even within us. You see, the woman of Samaria was subordinate to the dominant culture of Jesus's time, and she knew from her cultural tradition and wisdom that the Messiah was coming.

The Samaritans held the Hebrew patriarchs in high esteem, as evidenced by their veneration of Jacob's well. "Thus, for the woman, Jesus's implicit claim to be on par with the patriarch Jacob has enormous theological implications."[4] In addition, her people believed the Messiah would be the prophet promised by God to Moses in Deuteronomy 18:18–19. Sandra Schneiders, a New Testament scholar and professor, states that "According to Samaritan theology, the Messiah would be . . . a prophet like Moses . . . who upon his return, would reveal all things and restore true worship."[5]

That was cultural knowledge passed down from generation to generation. That knowledge helped to anchor members of this community, including this woman, to their cultural and religious traditions. Like my Granny shared with me, the woman at the well knew what she knew. And that knowledge was foundational to her receiving a revelation from Jesus. I find it marvelous that God uses much in our various cultural traditions to prepare us for and even point us to God's saving and sustaining grace so that we might thrive.

Too often, people from outside our cultures misjudge us due to their lack of our cultural knowledge. They don't listen for the wisdom they can find there. Too often, we have been judged as Black women for our cultural understanding and expected to minimize or abandon what we know to fit into the dominant culture's mode.

As Black women navigating patriarchal cultures and systems, we often learn not to trust our voice or that inner wisdom. We learn to second-guess it. As we try to fit into a Western, male-dominated system, we use the tools of that system, which feel foreign in our hands and hearts. By using the rubric of Western male knowing, we end up analyzing and overanalyzing and analyzing some more until we get stuck and lose our confidence to move forward with something we could access our way.

Some call this knowing intuition, and others call it instinct. My Granny called it discernment—that way of knowing not dependent on cognitive analysis alone but connected in the heart, gut, and spirit. In trying to fit into the mold of acceptable women, too many of us allow the loudness of outside voices to drown out the still, small voice within that knows and can guide.

Years ago, Dr. Collins provided four themes that comprise the collective wisdom of *our* ways of knowing that remain true.

Lived Experience

We know what we know through our lived experiences. "For most African-American women, those individuals who have lived through the experiences about which they claim to be experts are more believable and credible than those who have merely read or thought about such experiences."[6] That's why, deep inside, I knew that when Mr. Man tried to showcase his knowledge, I had the experience as a Black woman business owner that was going to resonate with my audience.

Your lived experience matters.

Use of Dialogue

We dialogue about what we know. As author bell hooks writes, "Dialogue implies talk between two subjects, not the speech of subject and object. It is a humanizing speech, one that challenges and resists domination."[7] We value community, and dialogue is inherently communal. Again, Mr. Man tried to move the conversation from a community dialogue to lecturing the rest of us, but that shift was unwarranted. As Black women leaders, we typically get suspicious of people who talk over us and try to overpower us with their words or actions. Our forebears toiled through too much for us not to be able to be dialogue partners.

Use your voice.

Caring

According to Dr. Collins, "the ethic of caring suggests that personal expressiveness, emotions, and empathy are central to" our ways of knowing.[8] When we care about a topic, we express it in our tone and our ability to empathize with our audience. This cultural notion of care is so deeply rooted in our beings that I was not even conscious of the care I was exuding by pivoting the conversation away from Mr. Man and back onto the audience of first-time business owners. It wasn't until later, when I reflected on the encounter, that I realized what came naturally to me flowed from this ethic of care for our people. I would not have them upstaged by a pedigree-flaunting white man.

Show you care!

Personal Accountability

Not only do we develop our knowledge through dialogue and share what we know in a manner that demonstrates our concern, but we expect people to be "accountable for their knowledge claims."[9] Dr. Collins continues, "Knowledge claims made by individuals respected for their moral and ethical connections to their ideas will carry more weight than those offered by less respected figures."[10] I don't mean to throw shade on Mr. Man, but I knew I had the receipts to show for twenty years of running a business that my particular audience of Black and Brown women and men needed to hear.

Don't be afraid to show your receipts when you need to.

Dr. Collins uses the Black church service, an experience many of us are familiar with, as an example of bringing together all four elements of our ways of knowing. The rationality of examining biblical texts is put in dialogue with the congregants' lived experiences to lift up the ethic of caring. She says, "Emotions, ethics, and reason are all used as interconnected, essential components in assessing knowledge claims."[11]

We know what we know. Let the church say amen!

· · · · ·

Let's revisit the Samaritan woman and her way of knowing. The Samaritan veneration of ancestors is why she'd asked Jesus, "Do you think you're greater than our ancestor Jacob, who gave us this well?" (John 4:12). The well was a touchpoint of cultural knowledge for this community. In her initial estimation, Jesus had dismissed this cultural anchor's importance. But he had not.

It strikes me that her relying upon her way of knowing took the conversation even deeper. You see, culturally embedded ways of knowing are much about surviving and thriving in our environments. Culture is a system of shared beliefs and values our forebears passed down from generation to generation. Cultural knowledge, including the ways of discernment passed on by our ancestors, is about seeing the world a certain way to help maintain our identity and facilitate our surviving and thriving.

Jesus knew this.

Transparency Begets Transparency

In response to her transparency about knowing the Messiah was coming, Jesus revealed his identity to her. "I AM the Messiah," he responded (v. 26). In so saying, he "disclose[d] that he [was] the expected Messiah and more—for the words 'I AM' ("I am he" in many translations . . .) link his very being with the one revealed to Moses in the burning bush (Exod. 3:14)."[12]

As Dr. Schneiders writes:

> Jesus confirm[ed] her intuition and reveal[ed] himself to her as not only the prophetic Messiah of Samaritan expectation but as *ego eimi*, that is, by the very designation that the Samaritans preferred for God, the "I am" of the Mosaic revelation (see Exod. 3:14).[13]

I can almost hear the woman now, thinking, *I knew it! I knew there was something about you!* Jesus validated what she knew. In like manner, the Lord validates what we know about the Lord's revelatory working in our lives. What had been slowly being revealed to her was now clear. The choice was now hers to believe that the One whom her ancestors had anticipated had not only come but had entered a dialogic relationship with her.

What does knowing mean for us? The Savior has also invited us into a relationship, given us the promise of a refreshing spiritual wellspring to remind us of who we are, and provided us access to resources of wisdom for our journeys.

Sisters, we know we will be challenged. Our authority and our competence are going to be tested, but we've also got to know that we know that we know—that we have a well of wisdom residing deep within that brings life to our leadership. This wellspring washes over our reactionary impulses and refreshes our minds and hearts to respond to the challenges of the day in wise and powerful ways. That is key. Women who lead well choose to respond to challenges from the well within. We don't react.

So, what are our ways of knowing that I am asking us to trust? As women of faith, particularly Black Christian women, our ways of surviving and ultimately thriving in our leadership contexts are through discerning, dialoguing, heeding our duty to speak up and use our voices, and demonstrating grace, care, and compassion.

Use Discernment to Lead Well

You see, using wisdom in the sharing of what we know is crucial to leading well as Black women. And one of the things we have got to do is call upon the wisdom figures of our tradition who, led by the Spirit, depended upon a way of knowing that transcended formal education and, in many cases, expanded their formal education. My Granny serves as one of those wisdom figures for me. As does Harriet Tubman, who knew that she knew that slavery was dehumanizing and wrong and galvanized every ounce of courage toward achieving her freedom and that of others.

I think also of Sojourner Truth, who knew that, as a Black woman, she had as much right and dignity as every white woman. She challenged suffragists to see her as an equal benefactor of equal rights with her famous "Ain't I a Woman?" speech.[14]

"Holy Spirit, Show Us What We Need to Know"

Dr. Debbye Turner Bell is an influential leader in the marketplace and in ministry. A much sought-after motivational speaker and former national broadcast journalist, she is probably better known to many of you as Debbye Turner, Miss America 1990, the second Black woman to win the Miss America title.

Debbye is a deeply committed Spirit-filled Christian who now serves as a pastor and continues to preach and speak. We met at a women's conference years ago and became close sister friends. Not too long ago, I invited Debbye to minister to the women of my church at our women's retreat, and she taught on the Holy Spirit.

A wise woman, Debbye shared many insightful lessons for women on leading well, and she made one point that stays with me still. She said, "Before I go into any meeting or new encounter, I pray and ask the Holy Spirit to show me what I need to know." She first received this lesson as a dating tip from her then-pastor Rev. Dr. Elaine Flake. Dr. Debbye has since expanded this mantra to every dimension of her life, especially her leadership. The Holy Spirit helps her discern dynamics that she would miss on her own.

Sometimes we don't know what we need or are about to face. Our first reaction may be to push through and handle what arises when it arises. After all, that's what leaders do, right? For every leadership situation (really, every life situation), we can go to the well and ask the Holy Spirit to show us what to do. It will help us to slow down and become more responsive and less reactive.

What Else We Should Know

We must know who we are and show up confidently in our identities and experiences. We cannot let anyone intimidate us with the games they are playing. And we can't let anyone goad us into defending our leadership or ourselves. We don't have to defend on earth that which heaven has already established.

We must know that we've been prepared for this very moment—whatever the challenge may be. We must know our audience and the value we bring to our audience. We also must know that wherever we lead or influence, it's not about us alone. It's about leaving people, places, and processes better as a result of our leadership, our speaking, our mentoring, and our work.

We must know that our voices are important, and what we have stored inside matters. What we say with conviction can rise above the din of opposition happening at the moment and will be what someone needs to hear.

We've got to know who is in our networks and partner with people we can trust to have our backs, as we will have theirs. There are enough of us out here doing the work of equity and justice that we are not in it alone. Other Black women and men know what we know and are ready to speak up.

Finally, in our most challenging times, we have got to know that God will show up for us. I think back to the confirmation hearing of Judge Ketanji Brown Jackson. On the hot seat and grilled aggressively by Republican senators on the Senate judiciary committee, she demonstrated for all to see a woman who knew what she knew. And I'm not talking about her knowledge of the law, her record, or the Constitution. Of course she knew all of that.

Judge Brown Jackson also knew the opposition. I'm sure she knew it from firsthand experience of experiencing resistance in her life to this point in her journey, as we Black Christian women all have. She knew and understood the political theater she had entered. Senators goaded her by accusing her of supporting child pornography and receiving dark money. Listening to the grandstanding of these politicians was exhausting for other Black women watching, including me. I can only imagine how exhausting it was for her.

But like my Granny had taught me, she knew what she knew, and she was called to this place for such a time to be the first Black woman United States Supreme Court Justice. The stakes were high, and she knew she could not let those aggressive senators bait her into reacting out of character. Our character is cultivated at the well of the Holy Spirit, and it was evident Judge Brown Jackson had spent time in preparation and at the well.

Not only that, but just when the exhaustion became almost palpable, along came Senator Cory Booker. When it was his turn to question Judge Brown Jackson, Senator Booker chose not to ask her any questions but instead to affirm her: "You are a person that is so much more than your race and gender. You are a Christian. You're a mom, you're an intellect, you love books." He continued, "You have earned this spot. You are worthy."[15] Those words resonated in the heart of every Black woman leader who listened to the hearings.

He knew what she knew, and what so many of us watching those hearings knew deep inside. Despite the mischaracterizations and the aggressive bullying tactics of other senators, Booker affirmed, "Don't worry, my sister. Don't worry. God has got you.

And how do I know that? Because you're here. And I know what it's taken for you to sit in that seat."[16]

When Senator Booker came through for our sister leader, we all felt that thing. His words moved her to tears. His words moved me to tears. God sent an ally to show what true allyship looks like for Black women leaders. Booker's support of Judge Brown Jackson illustrated the four interconnected dimensions of our ways of knowing as set forth by our sister leader Dr. Patricia Hill Collins. He used his lived experience and hers, credibly showing that he wasn't talking about book knowledge.

Senator Booker used a type of dialogue to speak directly to Judge Brown Jackson. He refused to interrogate her as his Republican counterparts had done. Instead, he in essence said, "Take a breath, relax. I got you." The split-screen video showed the dialogue of the heart—he touched her heart as the tears ran from her eyes, and she responded without words. Booker demonstrated the ethic of caring with his words and tone and took personal accountability for his senatorial power.

Sister leaders, I encourage all of us today to hold on to what we know deep inside. And as Senator Booker affirmed with Judge Brown Jackson, when faced with our successes that others try to diminish, when given opportunities that others want to label as tokenism, when others try to gaslight and bully us, we refuse to let anyone take our joy.

Hold on to the inner knowledge and cultural wisdom our grandmothers taught us. Hold on to that cultural knowledge that helped the Samaritan woman recognize the Messiah had shown up and come into her life. From that inner knowing, we can recognize that God has brought us to these places where we lead and will continue to show up for us.

Recognize and honor those God moments. We know them. Amid any hidden agenda or hijacked panel, God gives us grace and shows up so we can authentically and compassionately help those God has indeed called us to help.

Sister leaders, we know what we know, and we know we won't let anyone take our joy. We will lead well.

LEADING WELL REFLECTION QUESTIONS

1. Think about the cultural wisdom passed down from your family and ancestors. List a few wisdom sayings and reflect on how they inform your leadership today.

2. Recall a time when you ended up in the hot seat or someone attempted to hijack your presentation or point in a meeting. How did you handle it? What did you do? Based on the lessons in this chapter, how will you respond if a similar situation arises in the future? How will you prepare for that moment?

LEADING WELL PRACTICE:
PRACTICE GRATITUDE

In this chapter, I share cultural lessons of knowing I learned from my Granny, Dr. Patricia Hill Collins, and other Black women leaders. I am grateful for them. Find a quiet space and time to write statements of gratitude for your own key people and the lessons you've learned, drawing from your list in reflection question 1.

The following writing prompt may help you get started:

I am grateful for _____ and the following lesson(s) that help me remain authentic in my leadership.

SEVEN

LEAVE YOUR OLD WATER JARS BEHIND

The woman left her water jar beside the well and ran back to the village, telling everyone.

John 4:28

I was to cofacilitate a diversity and inclusion training program for managers and supervisors in a plant in Baytown, Texas, some twenty-five miles east of Houston on the northern edge of Galveston Bay. I was young and zealous to change the world, equipped with a doctorate in communication and culture, a gift for facilitating, and a lifetime of dealing with whiteness.

Typically, my cofacilitator was Bryson, an older white man. He and I were a good team, as we balanced gender, race, and generation. I suppose our strategy was to model how women and men from different races and generations could work well together.

Bryson could really challenge white men in their thinking about diversity and inclusion.

This time, though, I was assigned to partner with an African American man who was an affiliate of the company I worked for at the time. I don't remember a single Black or Brown face among the participants in the training room, and here we were, two Black "doctors" from Chicago as the facilitators of this program. I remember thinking, *This is not going to go well. Why would our training coordinators send two Black people into this hotbed?*

And sure enough, the tension in the room was so thick that my dad's special Thanksgiving electric carving knife wouldn't have been able to slice through it. We'd designed our program to teach the significance of corporate diversity programs, make the business case for inclusion, raise some self-awareness around diversity dimensions, and teach the skill of perspective shifting through a case study.

As with most adult learning programs, we had designed facilitation of discussion as the crux of ours. We aimed to help lead the participants into self-discovery of their blind spots around diversity issues, especially race and gender. We wanted to enhance the likelihood of them changing their mindset and behavior for more effective working together in more diverse workplaces.

I had gotten accustomed to pushing back on participants when they gave some resistance to the materials or models we shared. It was my way of getting them to think about the issues and their responses instead of just reacting.

Little did I know that I must have really pushed some buttons for one older white man who sat at the back table with four or five other colleagues. He seemed to bristle at everything I said. I'd been taught not to let a participant hook me—that is, to draw me into an embattled discussion that ultimately went nowhere and diverted the energy of the room away from the group and onto one person. But he hooked me all right—and my cognitive fuse must have short-circuited, as I honestly don't remember much of what I said. I do remember he accused me of painting him and his buddies as racists. "After all," he intoned in what I heard as his Southern good ole boy accent, "we have Black friends. In fact, I dearly loved my mammy who raised me, and we treated her just like one of the family." As a DEI professional, I know that being white, male, and southern does not automatically make one a racist, but in that moment, his drawl and mammy comment, erupted in my head to reinforce a trope I would have otherwise resisted.

The mammy figure is one of numerous cultural tropes historically used to stereotype Black women. Dr. Patricia Hill Collins calls these stereotypes "controlling images" in that they are used in an attempt to control the narrative about what is and what ought to be. "These controlling images are designed to make racism, sexism, poverty, and other forms of social injustice appear to be natural, normal, and inevitable parts of everyday life."[1]

The mammy image was used to justify relegating Black women to subservient support roles, and it stands in direct contrast to Black women leaders who direct, guide, and exert authority, agency, and influence. From the time of slavery into the twentieth century, the mammy came to be depicted as a round, brown woman with a rag-covered head who was the quintessential caregiver for white families.

You might recall "Aunt Jemima," a mammy character that was the face of the Quaker Oats brand of breakfast foods such as pancakes and syrup. Through the years, brand managers gave Aunt Jemima a makeover, removing the head rag and giving her a nice 'do. However, in response to the anti-racism protests of the summer of 2020, which called out structural racism and called for racial equity in all institutions, Quaker Oats announced it would be rebranding its image. Acknowledging the racial stereotype Aunt Jemima was based on, and even recognizing their past attempts to modernize the image, they knew the time had come to put the image of Aunt Jemima away and brand their products in more relevant ways.

We can't modernize worn-out wrong tropes. We must discard them.

Their press release said:

> As we work to make progress toward racial equality through several initiatives, we also must take a hard look at our portfolio of brands and ensure they reflect our values and meet our consumers' expectations. . . . We recognize Aunt Jemima's origins are based on a racial stereotype. While work has been done over the years to update the brand in a manner intended to be appropriate and respectful, we realize those changes are not enough.[2]

Sisters, each of us must do the same thing: take a good look at who we are and what we stand for and ensure the image we project as leaders aligns with our true identity and purpose. So many of us, in different points and places in our leadership, have had to fit in, go along to get along, adapt, and even assimilate. But at some point, in response to the uprising in our own souls, we must retire our old ways of leading for the sake of our overall wellbeing. To lead well, from a place of wholeness, we cannot afford to fit ourselves into the dominant culture's mold.

Now, back to my story. This participant loved his mammy. And this declaration was supposed to be evidence of his not being racist. I'm sure every academic piece I'd read on the mammy image jumbled together with my own personal affront at his unwillingness to even consider other cultural views in this training session. I must have thought, *The nerve of him. If he thought his relationship with his mammy could prove to me that every comment that has up to this point come out of his mouth wasn't evidence of his resistance to inclusion, he has another thing coming.*

Frankly, I don't remember how I responded, but I remember feeling at once angry and somewhat dejected. I wondered, *What's the point of doing this work if this is the response I get?*

Somehow, I got through the rest of the program. I remember leaving the training session and driving across a long suspension bridge over a brilliantly placid bay. The sun sparkled on the water. At the time, it struck me how peaceful the bay was, in stark contrast to the agitation that was rumbling in my soul.

Once back home in Chicago, I received a telephone call a few days later from the principal consultant and account manager for this large client. I'll call her Miriam. When I saw her name on my caller ID, I settled in for what I knew would be a somber conversation.

After our preliminary hellos, Miriam launched in. "Jeanne, I received a call from our client, and there were concerns about your training session in Texas."

"Oh?" I responded, standing next to the windows in my living room, looking out onto Lake Michigan some thirty-eight floors below. That's also how far away I had distanced my soul from that training session.

"Why don't you tell me what happened?" she asked.

I described my experience in the training session, and emphasized my affront at the mammy statement. She listened. Eventually, she responded with what I suppose was some level of coaching but felt more like she was delivering the warning one of her biggest clients had given to her. I'm sure she encouraged me to look at the issue from the participant's perspective and to consider what "mammy" meant to him. I'm sure I asked whether we were genuinely trying to work toward culture change or just checking the box.

In my estimation, the mammy of that man's youth could not be reconciled with the mammy image that derogated Black women. *For could it not be*, I reasoned, *that men like him would expect all Black women to defer to their white male authority in the workplace?* Isn't that what this man was bristling against in real-time in the workshop—a Black woman who did not defer to his white male authority?

After I ended the call, an uneasy feeling rose within me. "How could Miriam not get this?" I contemplated aloud. "What's the point of doing this kind of work if it isn't to get real change?" For quite some time, I sat with what had just happened. I leaned on my living room couch, staring at Lake Michigan on what seemed to be an unusually clear day, the brilliant blue of the lake reflecting the cloudless sky above.

Clarity likewise began to arise in my soul.

Could it be that I was a mammy type in corporate diversity departments? Was I hired to make white folks feel comfortable in their expansive training rooms with their fancy training materials, PowerPoint slides, and videos, so the corporate owners could check the box that they had offered diversity training? Could it be that I was expected to prepare and serve palatable programs like the delicious meals served on the plantations and not look up, speak up, or challenge the worldview or perspective of the predominantly white audiences who came to be entertained but not enlightened?

What was the point of diversity and inclusion training—or any education—if it didn't expand the thinking and perspectives of those who attended the program? And was Miriam as complicit in this corporate charade as the white women who'd looked the other way at egregious acts of violence against Black women on antebellum plantations?

Shortly after that conversation, I resigned. But I left more than that position. More importantly, like the woman at the well, I left a water jar behind. I moved on to another university position, so my move wasn't about leaving the workforce. It's not easy for any of us to quit our jobs, though every Black woman leader has got to figure out when enough is enough and seek the Holy Spirit along with other coaches and counselors for career-guiding wisdom. No job or career is worth sacrificing our wellbeing.

When we are faced with an opportunity or a need to pivot, we will probably find ourselves leaving something behind. John 4 describes the woman leaving behind the water jar she'd brought to transport the water she thought she needed when she returned to her village after her transformational conversation with Jesus. Once essential for the task at hand, it no longer had purpose *in that moment*. She left it behind for something different, better, and longer lasting.

The "water jar" I left behind contained a set of beliefs and expectations that limited me in doing the work I felt called to and that caused me too much frustration. I left the expectation that my white woman colleague would support me. Without leaving that constraining place, I would not have walked through the door to eventually launch my own company and position myself to lead well.

For us to flourish as leaders, it will mean needing to leave behind any water jars of assumptions and beliefs that hold us back and prevent us from moving forward.

The Water Jars

Water jars were vessels used to draw water from a well. Much like the pitchers and pots we use today in our kitchens, they were an everyday tool that served a domestic purpose. In the dry, hot climate of the Ancient Near East, water was essential, and water jars were a daily necessity.

On that fateful day, the woman of Samaria brought her water jar to the well, as she had most likely done every day before. This water jar came to represent and become an extension of her traditional role in her culture. Much like Luke's depiction of Martha, she was entrenched in household duties that, in patriarchal cultures, were seen as women's work. That is, until this strange Jewish man revealed his identity and his power to know her and accept her. As we read her conversation with Jesus, we learn of a woman who was much more than her traditional role displayed. We, too, are more than our roles and more than what others try to define us as.

Remember, the woman at the well left her water jar after speaking with Jesus. Womanist scholar Lynne St. Clair Darden says that, in so doing, "she performs the action of a disciple when she leaves her water jar at the well. . . . This act signifies that her traditional women's role has come to an end."[3]

Running to tell the good news about her divine encounter, she dropped tradition and picked up a new identity that influenced her community for Christ. We can do the same by leaving our water jars of tradition and limiting beliefs behind.

Could it be that leading well for each of us means leaving traditional expectations of how and where we live out our leadership roles so that we might bear witness to Christ in our own ways and our specific contexts? Think about it. Why was the water jar a detail that John included in his Gospel? After all, as Sandra Schneiders points out, the water jar is "a narratively unnecessary detail."[4] But it was necessary, because the water jar represented what would have been considered the woman's traditional role in her culture, and she left it to evangelize. The detail points to her dropping her conventional role and accepting a new leadership role.

Now, are we to believe she left that water jar for good? Would she still not need to draw water for her daily needs? When she returned with the villagers to meet Jesus, no doubt she picked up the water jar and even filled it before taking it back home. But I can't help but believe that now that she had spent time at the well with Jesus, she did not pick that jar back up with the same attitude or perspective she had before her encounter with him.

The water jar, for me, symbolizes the old mindset we leave behind once we have spent time at the well and are motivated to lead from the well. That old mindset carries the assumptions, beliefs, thoughts, and attitudes that keep us from leading from a place of wholeness. Like the unnamed woman who spent time at the well with Jesus, when we lead from the well, we are inspired, encouraged, and empowered to discard old, outdated mindsets and move forward with a new attitude toward leading well.

Mindset Matters

Let's explore this notion of mindsets more fully. A mindset is our approach to thinking about people, issues, problems, and situations. Through experience, cultural upbringing, socialization, or social modeling, we develop mindsets that shape our interactions with others.[5]

Mindsets are "habits of mind that [get] internalized."[6] Like water jars used in daily routines, mindsets are mental containers that hold the beliefs that guide our everyday interactions and are the bedrock of our identity. But Jesus comes to show another way. Sometimes Jesus challenges these bedrock beliefs, as he did for the woman of Samaria. Jesus expands our thinking about who the Lord is in our lives and what the Lord would have us do. Ultimately the challenging of these beliefs enables us to expand our thinking about what is possible and what God wants to do through us.

Here are a few beliefs that affect us as Black women who lead.

- *I need to be all things to all people.* This belief will cause us to get worn out and even burned out. We have a distinct purpose and group of people we are gifted to serve. It might be at our church, workplace, or community, but it's not everybody all the time at the same time.
- *I must please other people to be successful.* Too many leaders, especially newer leaders, try to please their managers, the people they lead, and their customers. We will never please everyone. Instead, we must focus on gaining respect. We do that by leading with competence, walking in integrity from our most authentic selves, and respecting those we serve.
- *I don't have time for self-care.* We must make time for self-care. We each have only one self to care for in this lifetime. Our most important resource is us. We must steward

ourselves well. We won't be able to lead anyone else well if we are not well.

Water Jars of Outdated Traditions

Traditions are part of our culture that sustain each generation. Traditions are also part of our faith communities and our workplaces. Leaders in each generation transmit practices and values to the next. But to lead well, we must recognize when it's time to flex the tradition. Then there are other times we have to discard a tradition when it is no longer helpful. We must ask ourselves, What are the traditions that are part of our leadership but are no longer useful or helpful for us?

One middle manager tells a story about a traditional leadership practice she learned from her manager that she had to change. This manager schedules monthly calls with each of her team members. It was customary for her to set the agenda for those monthly calls. She did so, as that's how her manager had done it for her.

Then it dawned on her that she was micromanaging her team rather than enabling them to participate in their empowerment. The water jar she had to discard was the belief that she knew what was best for her team members rather than listening to them share what they needed from her. She asked me, "Why wouldn't I let my managers determine the plan and identify the issues where they need my help? They know what they need help with!" That was an insight and shift for her in her thinking.

The traditional leader feels she has to be the person with all the correct answers directing her team without their input. Unfortunately, an unintended outcome of this tradition will be to distance ourselves from our teams rather than bring us closer. Letting go of that water jar will help increase trust and confidence among those we lead. We will be less stressed, and they will grow in confidence as we empower them to decide what they need.

Relational Water Jars

So much of leadership is about relationship. Leadership is an inherently relational practice. Ideally, we connect with the people we lead. We learn to trust them, and they trust us. Toxic relationships, however, can pollute our well and diminish our wellbeing.

I can't help but believe that Jesus's encounter with this woman at the well freed her from the cycle of relationships that no doubt affected her. She readily went to the townspeople with the message of the Messiah for whom she and they had been waiting. History and tradition have it that she eventually took up the mantle of missions with her sisters and her adult son.

As we saw in chapter 4, there has been much speculation about her sex life, but few have stopped to consider the effects those serial marriages and relationships must have had on her wellbeing. I can't help but believe that Jesus knew—just as he knows the effects of toxic relationships on each of us.

According to psychologist and author Dr. Elizabeth Scott, "A toxic relationship is one that makes you feel unsupported, misunderstood, demeaned, or attacked. On a basic level, any relationship that makes you feel worse rather than better can become toxic over time."[7] Toxic relationships can exist in "families, in the workplace, and among friend groups—and they can be highly stressful, especially if the toxicity isn't effectively managed."[8]

The water jar we must let go of is the belief that we must stay in relationships that have become harmful to us. As Black women leaders, we go above and beyond to help, to serve, and to provide. But constantly giving out and not receiving damages our wellbeing. We must pay attention to the environment we lead in and ask ourselves if it is a healthy one. Here are a few signs of toxic environments. In our leadership contexts, do we

- give more than we're getting?
- feel devalued or depleted?

- feel consistently disrespected or that our needs aren't being met?
- feel that this place has exacted a toll on our self-esteem?
- feel unsupported, misunderstood, demeaned, or attacked?[9]

Identifying each water jar is just the first step. Mustering up the courage to discard it if necessary is the next.

We must pay attention to what happens around us and how we experience it inside. Dialoguing with Jesus at that well, asking for the living water, discerning the prophetic, and growing deeper in her sense of worship prepared the woman of Samaria to recognize and receive the Messiah. That conversion of heart and mind was itself a discarding of internal water jars—a discarding of her old ways of seeing things—and embracing the truth of God.

Sometimes this conversion comes in our times in prayer at the well through the Holy Spirit. Sometimes it comes in encounters that reveal a disconnect between what our souls know to be true for us and the expectations of a situation or place.

I realize, in retrospect, that one of my water jars in my corporate diversity consulting role was my misguided belief that I could do serious justice work on someone else's project even if our values were not in sync. My teaching, training, and consulting flowed from a sense of calling (I'll discuss this more in the next chapter). I could not drink from someone else's well, nor could I carry someone else's water jar.

When I left the training session that day, I felt like a walking zombie; I now realize that this Texas encounter was an awakening for me about how I did my life's work. That is not to say other consultants are not doing great programs and helping people reflect on their biases. They are. Working with that team in that way was just not for me.

Once we let go of the old, we can decide to move on. The Lord opened a door for me to assume a faculty position at a university and serve as what in today's terms would be their chief diversity officer. Yes, as I wrote in chapter 3, I struggled with wearing multiple hats in academia. But I was getting closer to doing my life's work on terms that were consistent with my values. And I would not have gotten closer had I not discarded that water jar.

Grasp the New and Move Forward

As we recognize the mental and emotional water jars we need to discard, we each must take time at the well to reflect on our situation. We can ask the Holy Spirit to help us see our true potential and to reveal the needs we have the skills, abilities, gifts, and experiences to address.

We may need help identifying and discarding our water jars; that's where a leadership or life coach becomes helpful. Coaches help us articulate and reach our goals. They also help us identify the water jars that are no longer useful for achieving those goals and develop a plan to minimize or eliminate these barriers, which can be internal (our assumptions) or external (erected by others to block us from progressing).

Moving forward in our reimagined understanding of our leadership can be both exhilarating and scary. Moving forward in our reimagined version of leading well will truly be an act of faith and must be guided by the Spirit. Leading from the well is about leading effectively and leading from a place of wholeness that comes from the Spirit as we spend time at the well drinking the living water.

LEADING WELL REFLECTION QUESTIONS

1. Think of when you began to bristle in one of your leadership contexts, either a current context or a past one. What underlying beliefs motivated you to stay in a toxic environment?

2. Describe the environment. How did it make you feel?

3. What needed to change?

LEADING WELL PRACTICE: FROM LIMITING TO LIBERATING BELIEFS

Find a large glass jar or similar container with a lid. Get a pack of sticky notes or index cards in two different colors.

Card Set 1: Limiting Beliefs

Start by praying and asking the Holy Spirit to reveal any beliefs you hold that limit your ability to lead well. Using one color of your cards or sticky notes, write one limiting belief per card as they come to you. You may want to review the examples I gave in this chapter to get started. Place those cards in your jar.

Take one card from the jar. Examine it. Ask yourself the following questions:

1. How has this belief served me?

2. What does this belief cost me? Am I willing to continue to pay this cost?

Card Set 2: Liberating Beliefs

Using the second color cards, write out truths about your wellness, one per card, that can replace each limiting belief and free you to lead well. Search the Scriptures for empowering truths that can liberate your thinking around your leadership.

When you place the new card in the jar, discard the old card it replaces by shredding it, tearing it up, and throwing it away.

Continue examining your limiting beliefs and replacing them with liberating beliefs until the first set of cards is gone.

Next, begin building up your liberating belief system around your wellness and self-care by reading a card each day. Journal about the process of discarding limiting beliefs and replacing them with wellness beliefs.

EIGHT

FOLLOW THE CALL

The woman . . . ran back to the village, telling everyone, "Come and see a man who told me everything I ever did! . . ." So the people came streaming from the village to see him.

John 4:28-30

In my late thirties, I served on a panel for a Chicago-based career conference. The purpose of this panel was to encourage women to take responsibility for our success. The moderator asked my fellow panelists and me to address career satisfaction strategies for women reentering the work world.

I shared with the women in that conference that they could carve out a path that gave them satisfaction if they defined satisfaction in terms of their values and began to see a career as a means for following a calling. Though I led in a corporate space, my faith informed my approach to my career. I saw a career as a means of living out my calling from God. Even back then, I recognized that a calling on one's life was not limited to pastors and preachers.

God calls every Christian to live in response to the purpose for which God has created us.

When we see leadership as vocation, then our purpose for leading becomes clearer. As Black Christian women leaders, seeing our leadership as a response to a series of calls from God does a few things for us. First, it helps us recognize that our leadership is significant and a means to live out our God-given purpose. Second, we can see our leadership as a gift from God and see the leadership skills we have acquired as means to influence for good and make our part of the world better. And finally, recognizing leadership as a calling reminds us that who we are and what we do is more significant than any one position or job and frees us to follow the Spirit.

For instance, when we encounter difficult people in a particular place, and we recognize we've been called to lead in that place at that time, we won't let those difficult people push us away from our assignments. Instead, we remind ourselves that if God called us to that place, we are there by divine appointment, and no one can push us out of it for as long as God has designed for us to be there. And we must also recognize that we cannot stay in a place past the time God intends for us to be there.

Granted, the word *calling* is not often used for positions outside of Christian environments. But to thrive, we should have a deeper understanding of our roles beyond making money and landing big titles or corner offices. Our calling helps us align ourselves with the spaces in which God wants to use us. It helps us lead with satisfaction, through grace, and with humility—and joy! See a person consistently miserable at work? It's very possible they are vocationally misplaced in a job that serves God and/or them no purpose.

Seeing our leadership as vocation broadens possibilities for us as we align with God's purpose for our lives and follow the leading of the Spirit. As we lead from the well of the Spirit, we get clarity about our vocational calling, and we align with God about our life's work. I have found that Black women who do not approach leadership as a calling are most prone to quit, burn out, or fail to practice self-care.

Our Life's Work

When I speak of *life's work* I mean "the entire or main work of a person's life," as Merriam-Webster defines the term.[1] In other words, God gives each of us one life to live on this earth, and that life has a purpose. There is a reason God calls us forth into this world during this time and in this social setting.

Our life's work may also be called our *purpose*. At the beginning of this book, I mentioned two close friends whose passing deeply affected me and launched me into this leading well journey. One of these two friends was Dr. Chandra Taylor Smith, and her sense of her life's work and calling was profound.

I met Chandra nearly two decades ago at a gathering for North Park University, a liberal arts university on the north side of Chicago. That day, some one hundred faculty and staff convened to introduce new faculty—including me—and hold other start-of-the-year activities. I had seen Chandra from afar. Being one of perhaps only five African Americans in the room, I couldn't miss her. At the close of the gathering, I bent down to pack up my briefcase, and before I had even realized it, Chandra had walked up to me from the far side of the room. "Hello, I'm Chandra Taylor Smith," she said. As she stood at barely 5′3″, I felt like my almost 5′8″ frame towered over her. Looking down on her, I couldn't miss that wide-eyed, curious expression that would become classic Chandra to me. She asked, "So, what's your story? What brings you to a place like this?"

A place like this was a white evangelical university that aimed to diversify its faculty. At the time, it was one of eight Illinois universities in the Council for Christian Colleges and Universities, and North Park leaders considered their school to be moderately evangelical and more liberal than other schools in the council. This was to be my second attempt at working in academia.

"I'll be an associate professor in the communications department and serve as the assistant to the president for campus diversity," I answered.

"Oh, how neat. I'm going to be heading up the new women's studies department and directing the women's center."

It was no surprise to me that we both would be wearing two hats. I'd already learned that when institutions such as North Park sought to diversify, it was not unusual for them to do so by asking women of color to hold dual roles.

We served together on that faculty for three years and became lifelong friends. North Park was located on what some called the most culturally diverse corner in Chicago, at Foster and Kedzie, and attracted a culturally diverse mix of students from the Christian, Muslim, and Jewish faiths, as well as students who did not identify with a faith tradition. The faculty remained predominantly white, and Chandra and I, along with perhaps five other faculty of color, were the university's latest forays into diversifying its faculty to better relate to the mosaic student body it attracted. Our offices were in the same building, mine on the third floor and hers on the first. The work was rewarding, as we both loved to teach, but also exhausting, as we also became advisers, moms, and pastors to not just the Black students who readily sought us out for counsel and comfort but to all students who stopped by.

We would rush between classes to student advising meetings, rush from classes to faculty meetings, and then keep our office doors open for students to drop in to talk. At some point in the day, I'd usually run into Chandra as I was going to one of my classes and she was coming from one of hers or vice versa. We'd stop in the neatly manicured courtyard outside the back of our worn brick office building. I'd ask, "Hey, girl, how's it going?" She'd respond with a lilt in her voice, "Grace showed up today." That became our daily mantra when we'd see each other. The grace of God, personified as a woman who accompanied us on our grueling daily routine, always showed up to give us strength to bear what was becoming an increasingly unbearable load. Yet we were called there. At least for a season.

Chandra left full-time academic life before I did to become the director of College Summit Chicago. She sensed a call to College Summit to help prepare youth from under-resourced communities for college. From there, she held various educational leadership positions and eventually became the vice president for diversity and inclusion for the Audubon Society. In this, her last role before her death, Chandra integrated her passion for the environment with her love of education. "Jeanne," she told me as she was transitioning to the Audubon Society, "I believe God is calling me there." Her career, as stellar as it was, was at its heart a series of calls. Chandra lived and led vocationally, entering each new role believing and trusting God had beckoned her to that place.

· · · · ·

Parker Palmer distilled the notion of vocation down to *call*: "Vocation does not mean a goal that I pursue. It means a calling I hear."[2] From the Latin root word *vocare*, "to call," vocation is not something one hears from out there, amid the clashing cacophony of expectations demanding one's attention, but rather something one hears from within. A call beckons our true selves to come forward and passionately live out our purpose.

Yet we don't think of vocation as a call to our life's work or purpose. Our educational systems have diluted the notion of vocation by creating two tracks for students in high school: those preparing to go to college and those preparing for a trade. In my high school in Ohio, the vocational students prepared for skilled-trade jobs. They took hands-on classes such as woodshop or auto repair in the vocational building. The rest of us took our classes in the main building as our teachers prepared us for college. Really, neither track prepared us well for our vocations in the true sense of the word. Instead, they prepared us for going to college to get a degree that led to a job or going directly into the job market through a skilled trade.

I first became acquainted with the notion of a calling when I learned about those serving in religious vocations. For me, with my limited exposure, that meant nuns and priests serving in the Catholic church. This understanding of vocation was challenged, changed, and broadened when I read Parker Palmer's *Let Your Life Speak* for a seminary class. Let me tell you a little about this man, because what he has said about vocation can be eye-opening.

A prolific writer and spiritual leader, Palmer wrote that though "by all appearances, things were going well," he began to "wake up to questions about [his] vocation"[3] as he was trying to find his way in several business and educational roles. He, like many of us, yearned for "a path more purposeful than accumulating wealth, holding power, winning at competition, or securing a career."[4]

I have seen too often that if not taken from a true sense of calling, a leadership path can become the pursuit of trying to prove one's worth. For some people, the things we accumulate as leaders, such as titles, positions, and wealth, become proxies for our true worth.

We can take jobs and ascend into leadership roles because the opportunity is presented or someone else saw our value to their cause. Instead, we must see leadership as a call to serve and make a difference—a vocation. Leadership is not just about a title or position when seen in this way. And it's not the title or position that harms us. It's *how* we strive for the position and title that can make us unwell and place burdens on our souls.

All too often, we are pressured to live up to or lead into someone else's vision of a leader. In terms of vocation, Palmer says, "before you tell your life what you intend to do with it, listen for what it intends to do with you."[5] He reminds us, then, that to understand one's life's calling, we have to "listen for the truths and values at the heart of [our] own identity."[6] That's why we must affirm our identity after reimagining our leadership. Who we are is critical to our ability to lead well.

And even when we are listening, our life's work may not be revealed fully at once but rather unveiled step by step as we tune in to the voice of the Spirit within. The Lord has called us to follow, and we must proceed by faith, trusting the One who has called us. I believe this listening must start at the well.

Called at the Well

The encounter of the woman of Samaria with Jesus is a call story. Call stories are quite common in the Bible. It's in the everyday routines and busyness of our lives that God calls us. God's call is an invitation into a relationship, into service, and ultimately into a position of leadership.

In chapter 4 we explored how Jesus revealed what he knew of the Samaritan woman's life. Jesus also reveals stuff about us, though it often isn't about us initially but more about the Lord—as it was for the Samaritan woman. Later she proclaimed to the villagers, "Come and see a man who told me everything I ever did!" (John 4:29). You see, the One who calls us knows us and uses that intimate knowledge not just to get our attention—because it does—but also to invite us to follow. This piece of the dialogue operated similarly to Jesus's conversation when he called Nathanael, one of his male disciples, at the beginning of the Gospel of John. Jesus revealed what he knew of Nathanael's character as a "genuine son of Israel—a man of complete integrity" (1:47).

Stunned, Nathanael inquired as to how Jesus could know anything about him. Think about it: Nathanael had no Instagram or TikTok to garner a platform for others to use to get to know him. Instead, Jesus knew Nathanael before Nathanael could even present an image he wanted to share. The Lord similarly knows us, the true us created in God's image and destined for good works

(Eph. 2:10). When we don't yet know our life's work or what good works we will accomplish, God does.

So, to Nathanael, Jesus replied, "I could see you under the fig tree before Philip found you." In response, Nathanael declared Jesus to be "the Son of God—the King of Israel!" (John 1:48–49). Just as this scene with Nathanael occurred at his call to become Jesus's disciple, Jesus's insight into this unnamed woman's life ultimately led to the revelation of his identity and was the catalyst for her to respond to an inner call to share the good news about him.

How about Andrew, Peter, James, and John? How were they called? While walking by the Sea of Galilee, Jesus saw brothers Simon (Peter) and Andrew "casting a net into the sea; for they were fishermen" (Matt. 4:18 NKJV). Jesus called them to follow him, and "they immediately left their nets and followed Him" (v. 20 NKJV). Just as the male disciples left the tools of their everyday life to follow Jesus, so did this woman leave her water jar.

So many have heard how Jesus called Peter, James, John, and Andrew in their everyday working lives. Still, we don't make the connection that, in a very similar way, this woman steeped in a patriarchal culture encountered Jesus in her everyday life and responded to the call to follow and eventually lead. The call of Peter and the other disciples was made explicit, and in the story of our dear sister in Samaria, her call was more implicit. But one thing I know, whether it's made loudly or more quietly, is that we hear the call within us first. When our hearts listen to the voice of God revealing the truth of God's mission to us and unveiling that which our hearts have been longing for, we can't help but respond and run toward that purpose.

And that may be what the Lord is speaking to us today. Many of us picked up this book because we are leaders, but now God wants to call us to a deeper place so that we may lead from a place of wholeness. God wants to take our everyday work and transform it into our life's work, which can happen only if and when we spend time at the well and lead from that place.

How about Matthew? According to the Gospel writers, Jesus saw Matthew in his tax collector's booth and called him to "follow me" (Matt. 9:9; Mark 2:13–14; Luke 5:27–28). And Matthew got up and followed. Tax collecting practices in the time of Jesus were somewhat unscrupulous. Many Jewish people held collectors in disdain, even considering them to be sinners. In the minds of the community, the tax collectors worked for the occupying Romans and, in addition to the requisite taxes, exacted heavy fees for their services.

But Jesus took Matthew's everyday work and transformed Matthew's life. And Matthew was so appreciative of being called by Jesus that he hosted a great feast in Jesus's honor and invited all his tax-collecting friends and colleagues. What a witness!

What about us, in our offices? What might the Lord be calling us to do as an act of following the Lord that could transform our lives and/or the lives of others? Could the Lord be calling us to deepen our relationship with the Lord so that we lead from a transformed heart and have a transformative effect on others around us? Perhaps we already lead effectively. We make our goals. Our teams bring new products to market. Our ministry departments host transformative conferences. But are we leading *well*? When the Lord comes by our offices, what does the Lord see?

Does the Lord see a woman who leads by force, overtalking and overpowering others? Does the Lord see a heart weary from keeping up the facade of success? Does the Lord see us living out our life's work through our everyday work or just pushing through every day, trying to get to the end of the day or the end of the week so we can live out our *real* lives?

Pay Attention to the Daily Routine

The call from God doesn't always come from a burning bush on the backside of a mountain as it did for Moses (Exod. 3:1–10), or from a coat dropping from the sky, as it did with Elisha (2 Kings

2:11–13). The vocational call often comes to us in day-to-day conversations in which we don't even recognize the voice of God until much later.

It was in her everyday routine that the woman of Samaria encountered Jesus. This woman discovered the Messiah she and her people had been waiting for, and she left her water jar as those male disciples had left their nets to follow Jesus. This woman went and told the community about the Messiah. She carried the gospel before the male disciples did. We don't hear about her again in the biblical text. But we can learn more about her through history and legend. She indeed became a believer and follower of Jesus. And she became a leader. We'll talk more about her postbiblical story in chapter 10.

For her, it started at the site of the community well while she was doing her daily work. And as we listen in on her conversation with Jesus, we hear the questions she asked, which reveal a depth of inquiry. She asked him about things to which she had given much thought. Could it not be that, with Jesus, she could finally give voice to the murmurings of her heart?

Now, what about us? What are the whispers in our hearts telling us—that there is so much more for us? What are the sighs in our souls? Are they calling out to us that God created us for purpose, on purpose, and we can bring significance to so many people's lives?

We have got to pay attention to how God shows up for us in our everyday routines and beckons us to listen to the stirrings of our hearts yearning for purpose. That is where we'll hear the call to something more. It is in the questions our lives raise for us that we recognize the calls that come as invitations to serve, advocate, run for office, or accept a new leadership assignment. We'll hear the call through the deep desire within us, such as when we yearn to work with specific populations. When our hearts hear this call, our souls must respond, causing us to perk up.

In our leadership journeys, projects, tasks, and programs will catch our attention, inspire us, and ignite our passions. There's a leadership dimension to what we do in those tasks, and no one does them quite as we do.

We must also pay attention to the feedback we receive from others about how blessed they are when we do what we do. Do we have a leadership gift that others see but we may not recognize just yet? We have to pay attention and talk to the Lord about these things in prayer. The Lord has been waiting for us to show up at the well.

· · · · ·

I taught a foundations for leadership course at McCormick Theological Seminary for several years. This class was the first in a four-course executive leadership certificate for pastors and ministry leaders. The first assignment I always gave these leaders before class started was to reflect on how leadership had become a vocation for them.

Many leaders would write that they hadn't thought of leadership as a vocation until I challenged them to reflect on their journey. Many would write about how they'd emerged as leaders very early in their lives, recounting how they were called to lead school or church projects, or how they'd accepted leadership roles by college.

Writer, philosopher, and theologian Søren Kierkegäard put it this way: "Life must be understood backwards. . . . But . . . it must be lived forward."[7] We are living our lives, and we are leading. We must keep leading forward. But while we do, we need to take some time to reflect on the signs and signposts of life that the Lord has sent us down through the years. Leading well may require we adjust how we lead and perhaps why we lead, but not necessarily that we lead.

As Black Christian women, so many of us acquired leadership skills by being given responsibilities to tend to or for our younger siblings. Others started directing the youth choir and the mantle of leading fell upon us. Still others worked with the older women of our churches in the missionary society or women's ministry, and these women prepared us to lead.

And for many of us, leading became second nature—even if we didn't call it leadership. But now, in this season, God is calling us to the well to reflect, listen, and move forward differently.

Vocational Path

For most of us who will lead well, our vocational path will be indirect, as you have seen in my story shared throughout this book. Following the Lord's call leads us down trails that have not yet been blazed by anyone else. I know that was the case for me. I had no examples of following a call to develop women and men in and outside of the church as pastor, leadership consultant, and coach. But that's how I am living out the call from God to make a difference for good in others' lives. We may not have many role models or mentors on our distinct paths, but we will have the call of God and many confirmations of that call.

For instance, I had a call to preach and teach the gospel in what some would see as a traditional ministry. But I felt just as called to the marketplace to develop leaders and systems. I also felt as equally called to fight for racial and gender justice in the workplace as I felt called to preach and teach in the church.

I eventually realized I was called to advocate for women both in and out of the church. Oh yeah, I was a little uneasy with it at first. There were times in my life when I wanted a full-time ministry position, like some of my friends in the church who were doing traditional ministry things. Instead, I led in my local churches, preached, taught, and built a career equipping emerging and existing leaders with the tools to lead. I worked with corporations on policies and programs that advanced women and created more equitable and inclusive workplaces for women.

As we adjust our leadership to lead well and not just lead according to someone else's vision, or even the culture's expectation of us, we may not have exact models for what it looks like. Still, my aim in this book is to give us tools to sit at the well and listen for the call and the next step. Even after accepting our unique calls and paths, it will take courage to make the shift.

Vocational Courage

In his bestselling book *The Purpose Path*, Dr. Nicholas Pearce names what it takes to follow our callings to lead well: vocational courage. Vocational courage is "the boldness to faithfully pursue the fulfillment of one's distinctive purpose or life's work. It is about developing both the clarity and the commitment to make the difficult decisions necessary to align one's daily work with one's life's work."[8] Too many of us spend hours upon hours every day going to frustrating jobs, waiting for the weekend to come to live out our call.

Before I launched my own business, when I worked for other companies in addition to serving in ministry, I had to discern the company's fit. I had to determine the alignment of my God-given values and purpose with my role in each company. And as you have read, when there wasn't an alignment, I sensed the call to move on. Like the woman of Samaria, I ran toward my village—the places and communities in which I was called to share the good news of purpose and do so in a way that was healthy for me and those I served.

I recently had an insight that I believe came directly from the Spirit. In my work to develop women leaders and create inclusive and equitable workplaces, I was helping to tear down patriarchy. And wherever we tear down patriarchy, we're doing kingdom work. That's what I was doing in my own way, in my spheres of influence: tearing down patriarchal assumptions and ideas bit by bit, company by company—freeing women to influence and lead from their authentic selves and creating conditions in their contexts to give them exposure and opportunities to lead. That has been a crucial part of my life's work in and out of the church. The sense of call has sustained me in my unique vocation. And as more of us step into our true leadership callings as Black women, we will undoubtedly further weaken, in our individual ways, the walls of the patriarchy.

Get into Focus Mode

I love these new smartphones. We can put our phones on do not disturb and not receive any calls or notifications. Or we can put our phones in personal focus mode, and not only will we not receive calls, texts, or notifications but people who text us will receive a message letting them know we are not receiving notifications.

I want each of us to do that right now: get into focus mode. For some, this may mean using the focus function on our phone. It may mean turning our phone off or finding a private space. However it looks for each of us, focus mode means getting rid of distractions, both online and in our physical environment, and going to the well to talk to the Lord about our leadership.

It's time to get still and start listening for vocation—for what the Spirit says about who we are and the values we are called to live by. What do we need to do now to show up authentically in our leadership? We listen to the needs that get our attention, and we listen to how we have been uniquely gifted to meet those needs.

Another great writer, the late Frederick Buechner, defines *vocation* as the place where "our deep gladness meets the world's deep needs."[9] I love the thought of that: deep gladness. The joy that simmers in our hearts and souls and bubbles up to the surface when we are doing what we've been called to do from the place we have been authentically formed to be.

I heard the call to my place of vocation: at the intersection of the world's need for gender and racial equality, specifically in terms of women's leadership, and my joy and delight to develop programs and write. I was called to serve here. What I love about

Buechner's advice is when we find that intersective place that is our vocation, our service doesn't feel like work. It's what makes our hearts glad. It's what brings fulfillment.

After I began regularly leading Bible studies at one of my former churches, one of my fellow pastors remarked, "You were born to teach." Yes, I was. When I teach, I am honoring who I was created to be. And because I had vocational clarity and courage, I didn't allow myself to get stuck in any place that squelched that teaching gift.

Because of vocational creativity, I fulfill my call to teach through my business, church pastoral role, writing, and mentoring. I have served as a professor and taught undergraduate students, graduate students, and professional students. I have led radio programs that, at the core, were teaching platforms. I use my blog and social media platforms to teach. I can't help but teach to develop and help others grow. My leadership purpose is to move people and systems to higher levels of effectiveness and wholeness through teaching, training, and development.

Gaining Vocational Clarity

Vocational clarity starts with understanding and embracing our leadership purpose. Purpose helps us align all the various components of life (work, home, community) into an integrative whole that provides clarity and coherence to what we do in any given context at any given time. Our purpose is the reason we exist and lead the way we do. Leadership purpose can transcend a specific role and broaden our perspective for possibilities for our leadership. But leadership purpose is much more. Leadership purpose also provides the alignment of our why and our what. We each have many skills, gifts, abilities, and experiences. When others see how talented and gifted we are, they want us on their teams and can pull us into so many endeavors that we get stretched and miss living out our purpose.

Leadership purpose helps provide the boundaries to our life's work. It serves as the guardrails in our vocational journey that keep us from getting off track. Each of us will need to develop a leadership purpose statement. That statement is the why of our lives and leadership. It encompasses the needs directed to us by a particular group of people or place using the core values that guide our lives. Our leadership purpose statement will provide a good framework for the criterion we need to recognize which requests are in line with our purpose in that season and which are not.

We will also need to develop the discipline to stop saying yes as if on autopilot. And please hear that—if we are not good at saying no, we must start saying yes less frequently.

Spend Time at the Well

At the well, we develop our means for hearing the yes from God that overrides our tendency to say yes to everything and everyone else, whether it aligns with our purpose or not. So, there we have it. Sisters, we are so gifted, and our leadership is so needed. The world is waiting for us. But we need to be well and show up whole and healthy.

It is time for all of us as Black Christian women to follow the call to lead authentically and vocationally.

LEADING WELL REFLECTION QUESTIONS

1. What does vocational courage mean for you, and how might you demonstrate it so you can lead well?

2. What does vocational creativity mean for you? What are the creative ways in which you can express your authentic calling? In what ways does your current leadership model enable you to express vocational creativity? In what ways does it hinder your expression of vocational creativity? What does this mean for you?

LEADING WELL PRACTICE: LEADERSHIP PURPOSE STATEMENT

Developing Your Leadership Purpose Statement.

Use the following elements to develop your leadership purpose statement.[10]

A. Need-directed: A leadership purpose statement conveys that you are putting your leadership in service of Buechner's notion of the world's deep needs. That means some group or population is helped by your leadership. Whom do you feel called to serve?

B. Values-based: A leadership purpose statement will reflect your core values. Your values are those guiding principles you live by and are distinct to your leadership.

- Do an internet search for "core values list."
- Read through the list and highlight seven items that resonate with you and describe the driving principles of your leadership.

- Write those seven values on a sheet of paper, and for each write out how it speaks to you and how you demonstrate it in your leadership.
- From that list of seven, identify the top three values that capture the driving force of your leadership.

C. Action-oriented: A leadership purpose statement reflects the unique activities you provide through your leadership. What action words describe the core of what you do?

Pulling It All Together

Fill in the blanks with the words you used above for each element of a leadership purpose statement.

My leadership purpose is to (action words that reflect my leadership):

_____

_____

_____

_____

My core values are:

_____

_____

_____

_____

My group or population is:

_____

_____

Write out your leadership purpose statement using the above elements, placing the words in an order that conveys the essence of your purpose. Read it out loud a few times. Tweak it as necessary. Write or type it onto a card and post it where you can review it as you continue with this book.

NINE

LEAD ON WITH LIGHT

Jesus . . . sat wearily beside the well about noontime.
Soon a Samaritan woman came to draw water.

John 4:6-7

It was January 10, 2017, and my friend Wanda had made sure my husband and I had tickets to President Barack Obama's farewell address at McCormick Place in Chicago. A serendipitous meeting in the elevator with a presidential staffer led to us getting seats in the VIP section. The atmosphere in the venue that night was electrifying. There we sat, five rows from the front of the stage. Near the end of President Obama's speech, a woman next to my husband and I coached us on how to get down quickly to the stage and the security rope line so that we could possibly shake the president's hand.

We did it. Now I must say I asked President Obama to take a selfie with me, and he placed his hand on my shoulder and replied, "I can't do that; there are too many people in this line that I have to get to." Why did I even ask?

When Mrs. Obama stood before me to shake my hand, I thanked her for her service and remarked, "You represented us so well."

She looked me straight in the eyes and sincerely, without missing a beat, said, "Well, that's who we are." Her intonation led me to believe she wasn't just talking about herself, her daughters, and her mother but meant that is who *we* are as Black women. We can thrive in the most hostile environments and shine in the darkest nights. We can—and we do!

We represent God, each other, the community, and that which is right. As Black women who lead, who we are shines from within. We indeed are lights.

The Light

Light, in both the literal and metaphorical sense, figures heavily in Scripture. It is especially prominent in the Gospel of John, including in this story of the woman of Samaria. Light represents the essence of our character as followers of Christ, kingdom agents, and leaders (Matt. 5:14, 16). In the sermon about his kingdom, Jesus used light, along with salt, to represent the transforming influence believers have on our environment. Even more so, it is from this light that good deeds shine forth and glorify God. Our light in the world speaks of our penetrating influence for good.

Light also represents knowledge or spiritual revelation. For instance, in 2 Corinthians 4:6, we are told that the God who said, "'Let there be light in the darkness,' has made this light shine in our hearts so we could know the glory of God that is seen in the face of Jesus Christ."

For believers, the light of Jesus is life. Jesus declares, "I am the light of the world. If you follow me, you won't have to walk in darkness, because you will have the light that leads to life" (John 8:12). In his Gospel, John often contrasted light, which symbolizes truth and our call to be truth-tellers, with darkness, which represents "ignorance of divine truth."[1]

Be Clothed with Light

The story of this unnamed woman occurs at noon. Though we don't know the weather conditions of that day, positioning the encounter at midday allowed John to contrast this woman's story with Nicodemus's story in the previous chapter. Nicodemus, a member of the religious elite, came in the dark of night to ask questions of Jesus. But Jesus waited in the light of day for an unnamed working-class woman to ask her a question that would lead her to the revelatory knowledge of Jesus as Messiah.

In this way, John shows the inclusivity of the gospel of Jesus. Whether by night or by day, we can come to Jesus. Whether religious insiders or ethnic outsiders, we come to Jesus.

I love the way Lynne St. Clair Darden puts it: "Literally it is the Jewish male leader who operates in darkness, and the ethnic female other who walks not only in the light, but at a time when the light has reached its apex at high noon. She is the woman clothed in the sun."[2] Could this setting foreshadow the enlightened woman she was to become when filled with the living water of the Spirit?

The image of this woman clothed in light reminds me of Romans 13:12. Here, followers of Christ are admonished to "strip away what is done in the shadows of darkness. . . . And once and for all we clothe ourselves with the radiance of light as our weapon" (TPT).

We have the light of God within us, and we, too, must take up the armor of light and be clothed in light. These are all metaphoric and brilliantly vivid ways of saying that, as Christian women who lead, we must lead with light and hold fast to the truth of God in our lives and the truth of God's Word for our lives.

To lead with light is to lead from the values and principles of Christ, holding fast to that which is good, right, and just. As women who drink from the well of living water, we should see the light of God's love shining through our acts of compassionate service. As enlightened women, the light of God's righteousness must shine through our justice and equity work. The light of God's shalom fuels our passion for working for peace.

To lead with light is to advance principles and practices of God's kingdom that are in the best interests of the people we lead and the communities we serve, working toward the greater and common good.

This woman did just that. She left her water jar beside the well and ran back to the village, telling everyone, "Come and see a man who told me everything I ever did! Could he possibly be the Messiah?" (John 4:29). This woman was a light in witnessing to her village. She pointed them to the "light of the world" (8:12). Jesus had enlightened her about worship and his identity. With his truth burning warmly in her heart, she compelled the villagers to follow her out to meet Jesus. She was leading people to Christ. His male disciples had not even done that yet.

Sisters, we have the same opportunity. As we are enlightened by Christ, we can let our lights shine through our good deeds (Matt. 5:16). These good deeds include leading in a way that builds people up and does not tear them down and is mindful of the tone we use to speak with others, even when holding them accountable and giving performance feedback. They also include getting to know the people on our teams and respecting their humanity, and giving of our time, talent, and treasure to causes that help others.

Shine Like Mama Day

Gloria Naylor was a literary genius who captured many dimensions of the Black woman's experiences in diverse contexts. In her eponymous novel, Naylor introduced us to Mama Day, a Black woman leader who embodied this light. Though fiction, *Mama Day* speaks to all of us.

Mama Day was the legendary matriarch and a midwife on the fictional island of Willow Springs, part of the Sea Islands, which are a set of barrier islands running off the Atlantic coast from

North Carolina to Florida. The threats to the Sea Islands have been well documented: the darkness of resort encroachment, the destruction of the family as young people move away from the islands and their traditional folkways. Yet Mama Day, at ninety years of age, persisted in leading the community, fighting to preserve the land, sustain the culture, heal the community, and protect the island's legacy and her people. Mama Day led from an inner light that inspired others to shine and is an example of a Black woman leading in dark places "whose strength is rooted in her community and family."[3]

Each of us who are called to lead likewise faces threats to our leadership as well as to our communities. It could be the threat of ethical violations in our companies, violence in our neighborhoods, or policies that disadvantage Black women and girls. It could be educational practices that threaten to sideline and derail the futures of our children. I can't help but think of the video of a little white boy captured on a family's surveillance doorbell camera.[4] He came with a whip in hand, supposedly calling for the family's little girl to come out. Where does a grade-schooler get the idea that he has the right to threaten this Black girl, let alone with a whip, a tool of the enslaver's oppression?

That same week, an eighteen-year-old white man steeped in white supremacist ideology drove three hours to a Black neighborhood in Buffalo, New York, where he shot up a grocery store because he believed Black people were replacing white people in power.[5]

Unless there is an intervention in their lives, little white boys who believe they have the right to go after little Black girls with whips turn into white men with assault rifles who kill Black women and men because of white supremacist lies. Or they become political leaders who rig the system against Black people by denying them voting rights, church leaders who preach a whitewashed version of the gospel—or corporate leaders who can't find "qualified" Black women to hire or promote.

Yet even in these dark times, we are called to lead with light, knowing the darkness cannot diminish the light and hate will never conquer love. Wherever we are called to lead, we have the power to shine our lights and work to improve conditions for those we serve.

That is why I was so determined to leave my water jar of tradition in the company I spoke of in chapter 8. I eventually launched a consulting company through which I could confront the darkness of racism and sexism in organizational spaces. I tried to do this in a way that told the truth about interpersonal and institutional practices that hindered people of color, especially Black women. Leading with light means being real about racism in all women's spaces and being real about sexism in African American spaces.

Candle Walk night in the fictional Willow Springs was such a vivid example of holding up the light. Every December 22, the people of Willow Springs would "take to the road—strolling, laughing, and talking—holding some kind of light in their hands."[6] It was a community ritual of togetherness, a shining light of generosity that penetrated the darkness of isolation and destitution. A lot of older folks brought out real candles, "insisting that's the way it was done in the beginning."[7] Younger folks started using kerosene lamps or sparklers. I can only imagine if *Mama Day* were written today, even younger folks would hold up the flashlight app on their phones.

But here's the lesson *Mama Day* teaches us: bring whatever light you have. Each of us has a light from which we build community and ward off the darkness. And in Mama Day's story, that was the purpose of the Candle Walk. It was an end-of-the-year ritual in which neighbors "short on cash and long on pride" could get help "without feeling obliged."[8]

Those who didn't have much could get a little something from their neighbors. "Since everybody said 'Come my way, Candle Walk,' sort of a season's greeting and expected a little something, them that needed a little more got it quiet-like from their neighbors. . . . It all got accepted with the same grace, a lift of the candle and a parting whisper, 'Lead on with light.'"[9]

Sisters, that's what I see as the power of us leading with light. We are placed strategically by God to serve, to provide hope and help. God calls us to bring light into dark offices and boardrooms—into a darkened world. So much unwellness exists. The Lord calls us to lead well, not just for our good but for the good of the community and the world. As leaders, we can create systems that help bring hope in communities where there is none and build up communities where members are broken down.

I remember fondly the small town where I grew up, where Mrs. Elizabeth Carter founded and ran the Thousand Points of Light Center, named after President George H. W. Bush's Thousand Points of Light initiative. Mrs. Carter created a community center and community programs to enrich the young Black people in the neighborhood.

We lived in a town with a population that was 95 percent white. The education seemed to be 1000 percent white. Yet through Mrs. Carter, we were exposed to and embraced the excellence and light of our Black culture and community.

Many years later, when I graduated with my doctorate, my close friend Helen and my brother Joe hosted a graduation celebration at Mrs. Carter's Thousand Points of Light Center. It felt like every Black person in my hometown was present. And most were. Because just like it takes a village to raise a child, it takes the support and prayers of that village to earn a doctorate. I represented every person in that center that night. My achievement was theirs. They expected me to use my accomplishment to serve and pave the way for others.

So, like the woman of Samaria clothed in the sun, we shine. Like Mrs. Obama, Mama Day, and Mrs. Carter, we *are* lights, and we can and must continue to lead on with light. How can we do that?

Guard the Light

As Black women who lead, we must recognize that there is a great interplay between light and our inner wellbeing. Physical light affects our wellbeing, and our wellbeing affects our inner light. For some of us, this interplay is related to the effect of natural light on our moods, mental health, and emotional wellbeing. Leading well entails being sensitive to our whole being and understanding conditions threatening to extinguish our light.

The first time I felt darkness beginning to invade my mind was as an undergraduate in college. The cold Ohio winter seemed to pierce through my coat, but more importantly, something seemed to hinder the light from penetrating my mind. Yet I persisted, the strong Black Christian woman that I was. But I began to take note that I didn't seem as light-filled during certain times of the year, primarily in the winter. Then, a few years after college, my friend Helen and I went on our first vacation together. We were young single professionals and were too excited to travel to the Bahamas. Once seated on the plane, I started perusing the flight magazine and found an article that startled me. I nudged Helen and said, "Girl, I think I have this!"

The article described a condition known as seasonal affective disorder, or SAD. For some of us, the lack of light in the winter affects our brains. Though the specific causes of SAD are not known, for some the decrease in light in the winter triggers a drop in serotonin, a brain chemical or neurotransmitter that affects mood. This reduction in serotonin may trigger depression.[10] I started reading everything I could on SAD. One book I found to be tremendously helpful was called *Winter Blues*.[11] Now in its fourth edition, this book helped me to develop a strategy for continuing to lead with light despite SAD.

One of the reasons working for myself and running my own business has ended up being such a blessing is that I learned I had to slow my pace in the winter months to account for SAD. For years I used light therapy, and I exercise regularly, especially in the winter. I sometimes tease that working out gives me that endorphin rush my brain needs to help me to lead well. I've also had to eliminate eating processed sugars during the winter months, as it tended to exacerbate my feelings of depression. We each have to know what our bodies need to protect the light.

And as my business matured, I ended up scheduling client programs and engagements so that I ended my consulting travels by the second week of December and could take the last two weeks of the year for holiday vacation. I also didn't schedule any trips in January or February. Instead, I used that time for reading, researching, and developing programs. And then in March I'd ramp up my travel to more intense engagement; in the spring, summer, and fall, I thrived—professionally and personally.

For years, this is how I managed the light in my life. It worked well until I began caregiving for my eighty-eight-year-old mother during the COVID-19 pandemic while running my business from home. My low point occurred much sooner than usual that fall, so I sought the advice of my doctor. I'd been her patient for over twenty years, and she was a great listener. As I shared with her what was going on, she said, "Wow, you're working way too hard to manage this seasonal depression. I can give you something that can help you through the winter months. Come spring, we can wean you off."

My doctor's words, "You're working way too hard to manage this," evoked feelings of the StrongBlackWoman we learned about from Dr. Chanequa in chapter 3. I began to get comfortable with the reality that though I had managed SAD on my own for most of my adult life, now with the changing conditions brought on by the pandemic and caregiving, I needed help.

But what happened next brought tears to my eyes. My doctor began to quietly share that she had cared for her mother for fourteen years. She said, "My mother was a good mother and deserved to be cared for well." Caring for a loved one is another very distinct type of leading. I realized in her office that day that during the winter months, if I wanted to lead well and provide consistent, compassionate care, I needed a little boost so my anxious mood would not dim the light of love I had for my mother.

Now, please listen to me closely: I'm not offering medical advice. I'm telling my story and how I had to understand the relationship between the physical light and my brain and make appropriate adjustments each year.

I'm back to leading my business from a slower travel pace in the winter, regularly working out and using a light box. That period of caring for my mom while leading taught me I needed some additional help for a season. Most importantly, it taught me that it is possible to care for others with consistent, compassionate care without sacrificing our own care.

Leading well entails leading wholistically and understanding the integral relationship between body, soul, and spirit. Leading well also entails removing the stigma of prioritizing mental and emotional health in all its complexities.

Understand Our Shadows and Light

To lead well also means cultivating the character of Christ and remaining mindful that our light and shadow affect others. Yes, we can extend light *and* shadow to others. While Parker Palmer reminds us "a *good* leader is intensely aware of the interplay of inner shadow and light, lest the act of leadership do more harm than good,"[12] I must add that a *well* leader is aware of the interplay between inner shadow and light and incorporates self-care and wellness practices into her leadership to reveal and address the shadows, so she does more good than harm.

When we ignore our inner selves, our unexamined motives, unprocessed hurts, and unhealed wounds threaten to overshadow our inner light and cause us to act in ways that are unhealthy both for ourselves and for those we lead. That doesn't mean these issues extinguish our light, but we must attend to the interaction of light and shadow within ourselves. We can think of these shadows as assumptions we haven't examined that often cause us to move on autopilot—without reflective prayer or examination.

I have noticed a particular shadow we need to be aware of as leaders. It's common to hear women talk about imposter syndrome. This concept was developed by psychologists Pauline Clance and Suzanne Imes in their study of high-achieving women. According to these two researchers, "despite outstanding academic and professional accomplishments, women who experience the imposter phenomenon persist in believing that they are not bright and have fooled anyone who thinks otherwise."[13] In other words, this feeling of being inadequate can cause women's lights to dim.

Sometimes feeling uncertain is part of leadership—and part of being human. Yet through imposter syndrome, we can start to accuse ourselves of being frauds. That label exacerbates feelings of insecurity and uncertainty and threatens to diminish our lights of strength and resilience. I now call imposter syndrome a leadership shadow that requires not only the examination of our assumptions and beliefs, as we did in chapter 5, but also an assessment of the systems that perpetuate imposter syndrome.

Authors and speakers Ruchika Tulshyan and Jodi-Ann Burey say the goal should be "fixing bias, not women."[14] They continue, "Biased practices across institutions routinely stymie the ability of individuals from underrepresented groups to truly thrive."[15] Think about it: "the same systems that reward confidence in male leaders, even if they're incompetent, punish white women for lacking confidence, women of color for showing too much confidence, and all women for demonstrating it in a way that's deemed unacceptable."[16]

Those vague feelings of not belonging, if we experience them, aren't because we are not competent, prepared, anointed, or gifted. Such feelings may result from receiving messages we may have internalized that we don't belong or that we are too much trouble and don't fit in with the standard way of doing things. Those messages fuel a murky set of assumptions that threaten to overshadow our light. But we don't have to let them. We must stay aware and alert to the messages we internalize about our identity, worth, and competence.

We can use the Word of God to reinforce who we are and what God has equipped us to do. We don't need to lead like anyone else. We are not imposters or frauds but genuine, authentic originals created by God and called to serve in our distinct ways. We must also develop our light-filled support system—other women leaders across a variety of leadership contexts who together provide mutual support and encouragement.

Here's another internal shadow that can affect Black women who lead: when progress is slow, or we don't readily see a change though we are doing all we know to do to work for and fight for a better world, workplace, or church, we can get discouraged and lose heart.

I "met" Dr. Ijeoma Opara on Twitter. She's an assistant professor at Yale and director of the substances and sexual health lab. The day after the white supremacist terrorist gunned down ten people in a Black Buffalo neighborhood, she tweeted, "No amount of DEI training can protect Black people in America."[17] Eerily, I had just had a similar thought earlier that day. I pondered, *Is any of the DEI work I and others do making a difference?*

I am sure there are times that many of us as Black women leaders must wonder the same thing. Are our lights penetrating this darkness of hate? Does what we do make a difference?

When those questions arise, we have to refocus on God and what God has called us to do so as not to become discouraged or, worse yet, cynical. Those emotional shadows will threaten to eclipse our hope-filled light. Instead, we can remember what our realm of influence is and remind ourselves to be clear on what is under our control and what is not. We cannot change the entire world, but we each can influence our corners of the world.

Yes, I get angry about white supremacists who shoot up a Black neighborhood grocery store or Bible study participants at a church, or white men who hunt down an unarmed Black jogger they deemed didn't belong in their neighborhood. As a Black woman of faith who leads in the marketplace and ministry, I use my consulting, writing, preaching, and teaching platform to challenge bias, equip inclusive leaders, and proclaim the multicultural, egalitarian vision of Christ's kingdom (Rev. 14:6). We each have our own platforms we must use to penetrate the darkness of hate, division, and evil.

We also have collective platforms or vehicles for exposing the lies of injustice and evil. That is why we must continue to organize and to vote for leaders committed to policies that help us and don't harm us.

Internal shadows, if left unchecked, will lead us to assume we have no power to make a difference in this world or that evil is overshadowing good. Truthfully, they can also fuel cynicism and distrust, and tempt us to constantly focus on watching our backs instead of facing the challenges, possibilities, and good futures God has planned for us (Jer. 29:11).

So we must maintain confidence in God, whose "light shines in the darkness, and the darkness can never extinguish it" (John 1:5). Our light cannot be snuffed, no matter how dark the season, because, to paraphrase the traditional Zulu hymn "Siyahamba," we are *leading* in the light of God.[18]

Be the light needed in our world. Lead on with light.

LEADING WELL REFLECTION QUESTIONS

1. What are the things you do to let your light shine? Be specific.

2. What conditions tend to dim your light? What can you do to counteract those light-dimming conditions?

LEADING WELL PRACTICE: PRAYER WALKING

Prayer walking can be a restorative practice. Fast or slow, depending on your physical ability, plan a walk. If possible, schedule an outdoor prayer walk (though it can also be done inside, such as on a treadmill or an indoor track). Consider asking a sister friend to join you. Map out a safe route in your neighborhood or a park. You can also map out your prayer topics or allow your prayers to flow as you move.

Start off by paying attention to what's going on around you and in you. What do you see? What do you hear? What do you touch? What taste is in your mouth? What smells catch your attention? How do any of these make you feel? There is such a connection between soul and body that we experience when we move our bodies as we pray.

After some time of walking, transition into praying about the beliefs and behaviors threatening to dim your light. After your prayer walk, record in your journal what you felt in your body and your soul as you moved and talked to God, as well as any insights about your shadow beliefs.

TEN

LEAD WITH LEGACY IN MIND

Many of the Samaritans from that town believed in him because of the woman's testimony.

John 4:39 NIV

There is an academic success center at Cleveland State University for students who have aged out of or have been touched by the foster care system. Students admitted to the program are awarded the Sullivan-Deckard Scholarship, made possible through the generous donations of the wealthy and philanthropic Sullivan and Deckard families of Cleveland.

The center was launched under the leadership of Dr. Charleyse "Charley" Pratt, one of the two friends whom I described in the introduction of this book, and whose death in 2017 deeply affected my leadership trajectory.

Most people did not know that while Charley was establishing the program and the center that would become its home, she was also battling cancer. So steady and intense was her resolve to create something of lasting value for young people who were often overlooked, those whom she'd embraced and called her kids, that she pressed through her illness to lay a solid foundation for the program.

Establishing the program progressed even as her illness progressed. Her son Jarrett, a mentor in the program and graduate student at the time, worked in the program with her. She began to pass on crucial lessons and instructions to him to ensure the center's success and keep the legacy of fostering success alive.

When it came time to dedicate the center, Charley was weak but determined to show up for the dedication of what she thought would be called the Fostering Success and Leadership Center. Jarrett told me that so determined was his mother to show up, even in her weakened state, that she ate spoonfuls of peanut butter throughout the day to garner enough energy to attend the event.

That night, with university officials, the Sullivan and Deckard families, and students who would be beneficiaries of the program, the center was unveiled as the Pratt Center. Charley and her family learned that night that the center was named after her, ensuring her connection to the ongoing success of the young people she loved dearly and cementing her legacy as the architect of this life-changing program.

Jarrett now directs the center, and it is in the top tier of college success programs. To her dying day, Dr. Charley Pratt led with legacy in mind. And within the last few weeks of her life, she entrusted the continuity of the legacy to her son, and in peace acknowledged, "I've done all I was put here to do. I have nothing left to do. I'm tired and ready to pass on."

You see, leading well is not about the number of days we live but about making those days count and, in so doing, passing our gifts on to ensuing generations.

Understanding Legacy

The original sense of the word *legacy* was about sending forth a group as, for instance, ambassadors or envoys. The word stems from the Latin *legare*, which means to "send with a commission, appoint as deputy, appoint by a last will."[1] It was about sending a representative to pass on, extend, and disseminate the wishes, desires, and causes of the sender. In that sense, sister leaders, we are all Christ's envoys, as Charley was—passing on the will of the One who has called us. Leading well, then, is about being Spirit-filled ambassadors for the Lord's will in our leadership and all we do.

Eventually, the word *legacy* shifted to mean "property left by will, a gift by will."[2] When a loved one leaves an inheritance, they have, in essence, left a material gift to their children or others named in the will. In this way, a legacy is something that can be handed down from one generation to the next.[3]

As Black women who lead well, we must leave a wholistic legacy that is both material and spiritual and helps ensuing generations lead well. According to Susan V. Bosak, legacy is "about learning from the past, living in the present, and building for the future." She continues, "[It] is what is fundamental to what it means to be human," and helps us decide "the kind of life we want to live and the kind of world we want to live in."[4] Legacy is especially about the kind of world we want to leave for the next generation. We transmit value and values to those we lead and those who will lead after us. It is about purpose—that is, God working purposefully through us—and about vision. It reminds us that we play a part in the story of God.

Legacy is ultimately about the stories that get told about us when we are gone. It is about the testimonies of what we stood for and championed and what we established to advance the causes we believed in and promoted so passionately.

The Samaritan Woman's Testimony

The Samaritan woman testified that she had met the long-awaited Messiah. The people followed her back to the well, and many believed in Christ because of her testimony. Yet her witness didn't end there.

In chapter 1, I briefly introduced you to St. Photini, a woman venerated in the Eastern Orthodox Church for her missionary leadership and courage in speaking truth to power.[5] Tradition has it that *she* was the Samaritan woman at the well mentioned in John 4.

If you're like me, you did not learn her name or her connection to the woman at the well while attending Sunday school, Bible study, or Sunday morning service. Yet she's someone we should know, and her gift of leadership is significant.

Her significance in the Eastern Orthodox Church is great! Here's some background. Early in church history, two streams of tradition emerged: the Western church (of which the Catholic and Protestant churches of Europe and the Americas are examples), and the Eastern or Orthodox church (of which the Greek Orthodox and Coptic churches of Ethiopia are examples). This formerly unnamed woman is venerated in the Eastern Orthodox tradition as a saint with her own feast day.[6]

Orthodox historians have retained this woman's story. As mentioned in chapter 1, these historians, called hagiographers, used oral tradition to establish the history of the early church and prominent church leaders. *Hagiography* is the "biographical stories of the lives of saints."[7] I like to think of hagiography as the passing down of holy or sacred stories. As Black women, many of us hail from cultures with our own oral traditions, and we understand that hagiography is not history in the Western sense but is the passing down of stories and testimonies of notable women and men of the faith. Sometimes these stories are quite fanciful, yet the underlying facts of their lives and legacy remain.

Legacy as Holy Story

Saint Photini's story has been passed down through this oral tradition. According to Eva Catafygiotu Topping, author of *Holy Mothers of Orthodoxy*, like all "proper saints," St. Photini "has a legend, which begins where the story in the gospel ends."[8] Topping continues: "recorded in Greek collections of saints' lives, it tells the story of a pioneer woman apostle."[9]

After her transformational conversation with Jesus at the well, the woman of Samaria testified to the people of her village and literally led them to Christ. According to this oral history, she was then baptized at Pentecost. It was the tradition in those days and still in some Christian traditions today for a new convert to take on a new name at their baptism.

Through baptism, a believer is buried with Christ to rise into a new life (Rom. 6:4; Col. 2:12). This new name represents the person's new identity in this resurrection life. The Orthodox historians teach that the Samaritan woman took the baptismal name Photini, which means "the enlightened one."[10] The woman who met Jesus in the light of day became one who was filled with light. And as we saw in the last chapter, light is significant to shaping our understanding, our motives, and our thinking by the truth of God, as revealed in Christ and the Word of God. God's truth becomes the process, principles, and practices whereby we not only live our lives but from which we lead.

According to Orthodox tradition, Photini "converted many people, including her five sisters and two sons."[11] She brought the light of Christ to her family, to the community, and ultimately to the world. Indeed, having received the living water, the woman of Samaria was led by the Holy Spirit to what would become her life's work. Hers is a spiritual testament passed down to every woman leader who has been counted out, dismissed, or discounted. Photini bears witness that we lead as the Spirit leads us.

The stories of her leading continue. Photini journeyed "with one of her sons, sisters, and other Christians. Photini is always viewed as the chief figure in this missionary movement, despite the presence of mature Christian men such as her son Joses (or Joseph)."[12] With Joseph, Photini "went to Carthage to carry the gospel to North Africa. She preached there with 'great boldness' and won many souls to Christ."[13]

According to tradition, Photini had a vision of Jesus calling her to Rome. She traveled there with Joseph, who joined her in preaching and proclaiming the truth of the gospel. She is said to have confronted Emperor Nero for his unjust treatment of her fellow believers in Rome.[14]

Not only did she challenge this persecutor of her "co-religionists, but she tried to convert him."[15] From the platform of the gospel she was charged to proclaim, she spoke truth to power and protested the emperor's injustice, scapegoating, and persecution of Christians. Her actions join her to the long tradition of Christian leaders confronting empire through the liberating gospel of Christ. Wherever we lead, the gospel calls for us to confront not just individual sins but structural sin and its domination over the people God loves.

Photini's legacy reminds us that as Black women leaders of faith, speaking truth to power is part of the gospel call, especially as we protest and speak against the injustices our fellow sisters face today. The liberating, living waters of the Spirit move us to proclaim the same liberty Christ proclaimed and follow in Photini's footsteps to call out the injustice of national leaders and state-sanctioned oppression wherever we find it. Leading with legacy in mind also reminds us, as Black Christian women, that the Spirit not only compels us to speak up and out against injustice but to pass those values on to ensuing generations.

St. Photini's story is about the power of an obscure, unnamed woman who encountered Jesus at a well and was transformed into an evangelist, missionary leader, and empire confronter and was eventually martyred. Her story is about leading by the power of the Holy Spirit, the well of living water within her.

Her story, passed to us, is for us to lead from that same well of the Holy Spirit. When we lead from that place, we are more likely to create meaningful and purposeful systems and other things of lasting value. Legacy flows from the commitment to purpose and meaning, both now and for the future.

As Black Christian women, our leadership should reflect the sacred trust from the Lord to establish, cultivate, steward, and perpetuate things of lasting value. What we pass on, then, are the things of value that outlast us, things ensuing generations can use, extend, or build upon to further the causes of the kingdom of God.

Because an unnamed Samaritan woman showed up one day at a well outside her village and entertained the requests of a boundary-violating, barrier-breaking rabbi, we have one of the fullest accounts of the Holy Spirit in Scripture. She left us the legacy that Jesus indeed calls outsider women to reveal and disclose what God is doing in heaven's kingdom. And because she showed up and responded to the call to lead, we have Photini as an example of a Spirit-led woman leader in the early church.

How Legacies Get Established

Did the woman of Samaria set out to leave a legacy to the next generation? Probably not. But because legacy is ultimately about God including our stories in God's story of love, redemption, and transformation, our legacies get established as we follow the Spirit and the will of God in our distinct, individual ways. We lead with legacy in mind, not so much to ensure our names continue in perpetuity but to ensure we do our part to extend the work of God wherever we are placed. We pass on the values of God to those we have been called to touch and whose lives we've been blessed to encounter.

Black women both past and present have touched us, whether they were named or not or had a title of leader or not. In many ways, I carry on the legacy of my maternal grandmother, Nellie Bell VanLier, or Granny as my cousins and I called her. She was my first pastor and the first preacher's voice I heard in the church of my youth. She left a testimony of preaching and prayer, family, and faith. As a young child, I spent a great deal of time with Granny. I'd lie across the bed on my stomach next to her while we watched TV. Periodically I'd look over and see Granny, with head bowed, praying for her grandchildren. Following her footsteps, to this day I hold a weekly prayer call with a group of my cousins. We are extending Granny's legacy of prayer.

Perhaps a schoolteacher or a youth group leader touched our lives. It could be a college adviser saw potential in us, or a manager helped us navigate the company culture, or a pastor and women's ministry leader introduced us to the truth of the gospel that freed us from patriarchal limitations. Whoever these women are in our lives, they left us a treasure chest of hope as Black women. And now, we must leave the next generation with our gift: all the possibilities for leading authentically as Black Christian women.

I think back to my friend Charley. I am amazed at the intentionality with which she led with legacy in mind. She built a powerful reputation and brand in Cleveland through her corporate, academic, and church work. She operated in excellence that cemented in stakeholders' minds her value to things of value. We must ask ourselves, What are the things we are connected to or connecting ourselves to that have lasting meaning?

Ensure Continuity

One of the ways we lead with legacy in mind is to bring someone into the room with us and help them align with purpose. I mentor young women who aspire to leadership. One summer, my niece Kiara interned with my company, and I sought permission from clients to bring her to a few corporate leadership training sessions I was to lead.

One of those sessions was with a global client in New York for a leadership development program for women targeted for advancement into executive positions. Kiara came to assist me with the setup and observe. She got to mingle with these women leaders from all over the world at our networking dinners. And most importantly, she got to see me, a woman who looked like her, at the front of the room, and thus began to imagine herself in front of some similar room someday. Representation matters, and if our daughters, nieces, and mentees can see it, they can know they can be it too. That's leading with legacy in mind—not for us, but them.

My friend Charley's son, Jarrett, can attest to this legacy in his own life. "I'm not here now because I decided to be an educator," he said to me, recounting his leadership of the Pratt Center. "I'm here now because, as a child, she sowed into me." Charley and I completed our doctorates around the same time in Ohio; she was in Cleveland and I was in Athens. We regularly talked, encouraging each other and sharing insights about common readings. After we completed our doctorates, we worked on many projects together. Charley invited me to Cleveland State to consult on and speak for programs she launched. I brought her to Chicago to train and coach women leaders in my church women's ministry. Jarrett recalled my visits to Cleveland, during which he sat with us as we talked, shared, and strategized. Jarrett said, "I'm here now because she sat me in the room when you and she were talking."

He continued, "These are the words she told me before she passed: 'You have two reservoirs inside of you. You'll have to pull from the deeper one to do what you need to do. There is something else in you that you don't even have access to right now because you're not in the situation but when you get there, pull from that.'" Yes, sister leaders, we must draw from the well of the Spirit and wisdom within us. We must remind others we lead about the well within them from which they will need to draw too.

Create Space

When she was asked to launch the Sullivan-Deckard Scholarship Opportunity Program, my friend Charley knew deep within that to foster their success, these young people were going to need more than scholarship money for tuition, room, board, and books. The monetary funds were necessary, especially for underresourced students. But when a young person ages out of foster care,

> adjusting to life as an adult can be an unusually steep uphill climb—especially if they want to go to college. Personal and financial support are just the tip of the iceberg. For some, pursuing a degree feels overwhelming, if not completely out of reach.[16]

These students would need a safe space in which to grow, one that would be part of their healing from the trauma experienced in much of their young lives and help them move away from the societally induced stigma of foster care. They would need a safe space in which to connect with mentors and guides who could advocate on their behalf and protect them from the predatory inclinations of those seeking to take advantage of young people who have no parents to protect them.

The Pratt Center was established to create such a space. It strives to enable these young people to be well and places them on a journey toward wholeness. It allows for "those real-life living experiences that young people don't get in the classroom and gives people the capacity and agency to be able to grow in ways that can't be measured in grades."[17] It is a safe place for young people to be honest about their needs and, through wise mentoring relationships, coached to shift from a deficit mindset to believing that what they need will be there when they need it.

Many of us may not get a center named after us like my friend Charley, but each of us has the capacity now to create space for the legacy we want to pass on to others. At the heart of that legacy is the story we are living out right now. But sometimes we are so busy leading that we fail to take note in the moment of the significance of our own stories.

As with everything else related to leading well, legacy is about being present in the moment to the movement of the Spirit in our lives. The Spirit guides us to offer our gifts in service to God's plans and purposes for us. The earlier we grasp this truth, the better. None of us wants to get to a point in life where we realize we offered our leadership gifts to things with no lasting value—things of no significance.

Recently I served on a panel for a leadership conference hosted by the Building Self Determination Workforce Development program associated with the Arthur M. Brazier Foundation (BSD/AMB) in Chicago's Woodlawn neighborhood. The conference conveners asked us to name a person we thought was a great leader and explain why that person was so great. The panelists mentioned many powerful people, and the virtual audience started adding even more names to the chat. This list included titans of business such as Ursula Burns (the first Black woman CEO of a Fortune 500 company) and Ken Chenault (former CEO of American Express), historical figures such as Ida B. Wells (whose journalism brought attention to the lynching of Black people), and women and men from pop culture and entertainment, such as Mary J. Blige. Of course, all these people are great leaders for various reasons.

Mrs. Coretta Scott King is the leader who came to mind for me. She was the architect of a legacy—not just for her husband, Dr. Martin Luther King Jr., but for herself as a Black woman of faith who envisioned, advocated for, and enacted values of the Beloved Community for most of her life.[18]

Many people don't realize that Coretta Scott was already an activist when she met her future husband. She was "active in racial justice politics and the peace movement before marrying Martin King."[19] According to author and professor Dr. Barbara Ransby, when Coretta married Martin in 1953, though "she took on the role of wife and mother . . . she never abandoned her political beliefs or moral convictions."[20] She never lost her own "sense of purpose and determination that was all her own" and "the real strength of her character . . . is perhaps best evident in the work she did and the stances she took after her husband's death."[21]

That work was legacy-building work. Mrs. Coretta Scott King founded the Martin Luther King Jr. Center in Atlanta to cement Dr. King's principles of nonviolence, global peace activism, global human rights, and women's equal rights. The Center continues to do exceptional work in advancing Dr. King's legacy and providing critical training in the area of nonviolent resistance.

Leadership Legacy

I want each of us to take a moment and think about the people, processes, and places dear to us as Black women leaders of faith. We influence others by our presence and our passion. There are places in which we are depositing our values by how we lead and what we teach and coach. These things will become part of our legacies.

I started studying and writing about leadership over twenty-five years ago. In my early days, I noted that women, especially Black women, were left out of the leadership discourse—the formal writing of leadership theory and practice. That has changed, but not nearly enough to capture the vast leadership contributions of Black women in so many fields.

Legacy is ultimately about the stories of service that get passed on about us. We have the opportunity, as women who lead with legacy in mind, to start shaping those stories now. We each have the privilege of affecting how historians, family tree researchers, colleagues, eulogists, and others talk about us and the things of value we want to pass on.

In many ways, our legacies aren't just about us. Our legacies are about how our stories have become part of God's redemptive and transforming story for humanity. Each of us plays our role in God's story.

Here are some ways for us to start crafting our own stories.

Listen for Our Stories

We must slow down enough to listen to our heart stories—those things of lasting value for which we stand, create, and live. They reside inside of us now, but when shared, they can also bless others. Some people come to us for advice, support, and guidance. That wisdom is part of our stories. We have learned lessons through living and overcoming that somebody else needs to hear.

Own Our Stories

Our stories are ours to own—the good and the bad. Our stories are the compilation of the experiences and events that have shaped us to be the women of God we have become. They recount the significant events of our lives, the lessons we've learned, and our leadership journey. Each of us has struggled, and we don't have to minimize or negate the difficulties in our journeys or what others may see as the negatives of our lives. We can tell the truth and know that our stories are valuable because we are valuable.

Share Our Stories

In chapter 4, I mentioned that narratives support a perspective about events and people. For too long, others have created a narrative about Black women leaders. It is time for more of us to share our stories, control the narrative about us, and share principles and practices of leading well with the next generation. We share our stories when we step to another Black woman and aid her as she navigates racialized environments.

Writing our stories is also a way to share them. Even if you never want to write a book, writing your story in a letter, booklet, or other form can help preserve your legacy.

Jesus came to the well weary and asked this woman of Samaria for a drink. She had something to offer, something that Jesus needed. Similarly, Black women leaders have something to offer in a world weary of racism, sexism, and classism that routinely holds people back from having their own experiences at a life-giving well. Could it be that Jesus has met us at this well to remind us of our deep spiritual reservoirs and to stir us to leave behind our water jars of conformity and lead authentically as Black women at this moment? Is Jesus calling out to us to challenge others to change the narrative of our identity in Christ and join in the work of calling out modern-day Neros or structures that oppress, minimize, and dehumanize? The world needs us, and it needs us to lead well.

Many of us as Black Christian Women inherited a "legacy of strength"[22] from our mothers, grandmothers, and other significant women in our lives. And to be honest, we will continue to pass on stories of strength and resilience. We must. My prayer, though, is that alongside this legacy of strength we also pass on a legacy of self-care. We must leave a legacy of wholeness and wellness that includes an inner strength drawn from the well within that sustains us for the long run.

LEADING WELL REFLECTION QUESTIONS

1. Who are the Black women of faith who have influenced you and whose legacy you carry forth in some way?

2. What are you connected to or connecting yourself to that has lasting meaning?

LEADING WELL PRACTICE: WRITE YOUR LEADERSHIP LEGACY LETTER

Carve out a quiet place to begin to write your leadership legacy letter. This is a letter containing your perspective on what you want to leave the next generation of Black women in terms of leadership.

Who are the people to whom you want to leave a leadership legacy?

1. Who tends to come to you for advice, support, or guidance? What lessons have you learned through just living and overcoming that somebody else needs to hear?

2. In what places are you depositing your values by the way you lead and what you teach and coach?

3. What core values do you want to pass on to the next generation of leaders that will help them lead well and break through barriers they are confronted with?

4. What are the things of lasting value that you stand for, that you create, that you live for?

5. What are the key lessons you will pass on? What wisdom on leading well will you share?

After you've written your letter, make two copies. File one copy in a safe place, along with your other legacy documents such as wills and insurance policies. Schedule the second one to be emailed to you one year later. When you receive your leadership legacy email the following year, please review it to see how close you are to living out your legacy now. Then update it with new insights and replace it in your legacy file.

CLOSING

The importance of leading well and leaving a legacy of wholeness often becomes paramount when we face the mortality of those we love. While I was making the final edits to this book, the Lord called my mother home to her eternal rest.

What started many years ago as my journey into wholistic leadership evolved. At the same time, I served as my mother's caregiver for the last two years of her life. It was then that I came to embrace the significance of leading well, and I had to put these principles into practice one day at a time.

Even before her death, I began to reimagine my leadership and the additional changes I would need to make as my mother's health began to wane. I had already made plans to downsize my business to focus once again on women's leadership development and to not renew client contracts for business not related to my newly imagined vision of my work at this juncture of my life. In affirming my identity as a Black woman loved by God, I doubled down on my commitment to help other Black women affirm their identity and celebrate their leadership gifts.

During this time, I went to the well for strength to move forward and, quite honestly, to make sense of the timing of my mother's death. Though she had numerous chronic health challenges and had just been in the hospital for a routine procedure, there was no indication that her death was imminent. Yes, this powerful, usually poised leader fell apart as my mother died suddenly in my presence. For the next few days, I questioned the Lord, much as the woman of Samaria queried Jesus. And time and again, the Holy Spirit spoke peace into my spirit. The Spirit is still speaking to and helping me.

As I've noted throughout this book, as Black women leaders, we are expected to be StrongBlackWomen. I learned during this recent season of loss that the most remarkable defiance of that stereotype for me was to choose to tend to my whole being. I chose to be vulnerable with clients and share my loss of my mother. The amount of empathy I received was staggering, from clients sharing their stories of care and loss, to clients understanding my request to reschedule, to one client insisting we cancel all meetings for an additional week after my mother's Celebration of Life. Upon learning that I had kept my commitment to lead a session of one company's leaders, the executive HR leader took me aside and shared her caregiving story. Sisters, leading well entails leading from a whole place: spirit, soul, and body. And that means showing up authentically in our physical body, with our spiritual self, embracing all our emotions. Doing so gives others permission to be authentic too.

Authentically, I cried. Every tear I shed was in remembrance of my great love for Mom and an expression of the indescribable pain of loss I was experiencing. I know some leaders abide by the patriarchal model "It's not cool to cry." For me, I wept . . . and attended to some rescheduling to give myself space to be well and to spend more time at the well.

During this time of worshiping at the well, I perceived that the space I had begun to carve out in order to expand the care I could give my mother was now intended for my own care. As I made Spirit-led decisions about which clients to keep and which to drop, I trusted my deep sense of knowing and didn't succumb to guilt about leaving certain client relationships that were coming to an end.

In fact, I began to realize that, once again, I had another water jar to leave behind. It was time to transition from DEI consulting. Through this jar, I had served well for many years, but now it was time to exchange it for a new dimension of my vocation. The Lord was leading me to follow the call to the next phase of my leadership journey. I was willing—and ready to pivot again.

As the darkness of death settled and I moved through those dark nights, the light of God's love penetrated the grief of losing my mother and assured me of God's grace. And this book and others will be part of our legacy for the next generation of Black women who lead. Mom would be thrilled, I know.

Now Is the Time

Sisters, as you see from my story, leading well includes change. The principles and practices of leading well I shared in this book must become a way of living through the seasons of our lives. There is no perfect time to start leading well. Still, the sooner you start, the better you will be positioned to prioritize your wholeness and wellbeing as you lead.

Our lives are complex and filled with great uncertainty. And sometimes, as leaders, we latch on to a leadership approach designed in our minds to increase our certainty and give us more control. But often, that grasp for control only increases our stress. But once we start leading well, attending to our whole being as integral to our leadership, we'll find ourselves moving through life with a different rhythm.

When the woman at the well left her water jar and went to tell her village about Jesus, back at the well, Jesus had a conversation with his disciples. Without mentioning his interaction with her, Jesus began to tie that interaction to his broader mission. That's instructive for us.

The disciples asked Jesus to eat. They had, after all, gone into the village to secure food for him. Jesus replied, "I have a kind of food you know nothing about" (John 4:32).

Of course, his disciples were perplexed, not realizing they were thinking at a natural level and Jesus was speaking spiritually. Notice the pattern here was the same one he used with the woman of Samaria—and uses with us.

The Lord often has to remind us that as born-again, Spirit-led believers, we live in two realms. We see in the natural, but we walk by faith in the spiritual realm. That's why Colossians 3:1 says, "Since, then, you have been raised with Christ, set your hearts on things above, where Christ is, seated at the right hand of God" (NIV). Along those same lines, the apostle Paul tells us that "God raised us up with Christ and seated us with him in the heavenly realms in Christ Jesus" (Eph. 2:6 NIV).

So, Jesus clarified things for the people in the back: "My nourishment," he said, "comes from doing the will of God, who sent me, and from finishing his work" (John 4:34). Sisters, ultimately leading well, leading from a spiritually healthy and whole place, is about being positioned to do the will of God. God has a purpose and plan for each of us, and the well provides the nourishment we need to discern God's will and live it out.

Jesus continued, "Wake up and look around. The fields are already ripe for harvest" (v. 35). The woman of Samaria told her villagers about Jesus. Many came to Jesus and believed in him as the "Savior of the world" (v. 42) due to her witness and Jesus's own words.

I believe if we listen closely enough in this season, we can hear the Lord saying something similar to us. It's time to bring our whole selves into our life's work and follow that call wherever it may lead. The world needs what we've been gifted with to offer— and which reflects the light of Christ.

This is our season as Black women. Wake up!

The fields in which we lead are already ripe for harvest—for the fruit of a new type of leadership. A leadership that prioritizes our wellness and that of the people we lead. A leadership that cultivates an environment in which all can thrive. And ultimately, a type of leadership in which we show up authentically as women of God and lead others to show up as their authentic best selves too. That is truly legacy-building leadership.

Moving Forward

Reading and working through this book has allowed us to examine and reimagine our leadership. I've encouraged practices that enable us to lead from a place of wholeness: our entire body, soul, and spirit becoming aligned. In other words, wherever we lead, we can show up in our physical bodies as the beautiful Black women we are. We can show up guided by the spiritual discernment that comes from spending time at the well of the Holy Spirit. We can show up in touch with all of our emotions, not masking them to live up to someone else's stereotype of who we should be. We can show up mindful of the people we lead and create a light-filled environment for them to be all they can be too.

In working through this book, I hope each of us has seen that leading well is also about sensing leadership as vocation and heeding a call to lead from our whole selves. Perhaps that is something many of us still must sit with. As we grapple with this sense of call, our leadership purpose will become clearer.

Sister leaders, let's be real though. If we are going to see significant change in this season, we will need to be honest with ourselves. Too often we find ourselves in leadership positions as mere jobs. But when we come to embrace leading as our life's work or vocation, then we can more freely and authentically follow the Spirit in our leading. Leading well is about living out our callings through the leadership roles God allows us take. That may be revelatory for many of us.

The woman of Samaria did not stay riveted after she received her revelation about Christ. Instead, she moved on. She moved forward. She lived out her calling. So must we.

Here's how we can move forward together.

First, I commend you for reading and working through this book. I thank you too.

Second, I ask you to commit to leading well. Review your notes for each chapter and the end-of-chapter activities and form your plan. At the end of this concluding chapter is a template you can use to develop a rhythm for putting these practices into place. These leading well practices can help position you at the well to hear from the Lord. Review your plans weekly and adjust where needed.

Now, I commission you as *Leading Well* advocates. Let's share the message of leading well. Let's cultivate lived experiences around the messages in these pages. Let's dare to lead well by daring to be authentically whole.

As women of faith, we don't have to lead as the patriarchal world does. We can defy those structures and influence a healthier approach to leadership. We can start our own businesses and develop practices that enable us and those we lead to lead from a place of wholeness. We can speak, train, and teach leading well principles to other women and men.

We can start a revolution that enables more of us to live and lead well for the long haul.

Dr. Maya Angelou once said, "Each of us has the right, that possibility, to invent ourselves daily. If a person does not invent herself, she will be invented. So, to be bodacious enough to invent ourselves is wise."[1]

It's up to us to be bodacious enough to invent ourselves as whole leaders who lead from the well. Let's be bodacious in leading well!

Let's be bodacious Black women.

APPENDIX

LEADING WELL PLAN

Each chapter has ended with a leading well practice to complete. I now invite us to integrate these practices into our leadership to reinforce the lessons from this book. These practices are designed to help us slow down, visit the well, and position ourselves to hear from the Holy Spirit about our leadership and the people and contexts in which we lead.

The following chart is a summary of each of the leading well dimensions first introduced at the beginning of this book, along with the chapter in which the leading well practice associated with that dimension appears. I also provide a summary of the insight from the book in relation to each practice, along with the practice or practices associated with that dimension.

In the fifth column of this chart, I invite you to develop a rhythm for doing this practice that works for you. The rhythm can be daily (or multiple times a day), weekly, monthly, or annually. The key will be to develop your leading well plan and follow these practices.

I encourage you to review your plan on a regular basis and take notes on your experience. Which practices tend to serve you better for accessing the Spirit for strategy and gaining clarity in your leadership? Which ones help you maintain a sense of peace? Which ones do you need to tweak and adapt more for your life and leadership?

Leading Well (LW) Dimension	Chapter(s)	Insights from LW	LW Practice	Rhythm (Frequency for This Practice)	Notes
Spiritual	3	Deep breathing can calm your nervous system and can help you access the peace the Spirit brings.	Practicing breath prayer		
		We must break from our work, so our work does not break us.	Sabbath keeping		
	5	Worship can help you access the living water of the Holy Spirit.	Listening to your worship playlist Participating in corporate worship		
Personal/Identity	2	Affirming your identity can reinforce your agency to lead using your God-given gifts and skills.	Affirming your "I am" statements		

Leading Well (LW) Dimension	Chapter(s)	Insights from LW	LW Practice	Rhythm (Frequency for This Practice)	Notes
Relational	4	Understanding and accepting the relationship between structural biases (often expressed through work relationships) and your wellbeing is critical. Cultivating a community of allies is helpful.	Journaling to express your experiences Cultivating and connecting with your community of allies		
	10	We must leave a legacy of leading well for the next generation of leaders in our lives.	Writing a leadership legacy letter for the next generation		
Cultural	6	Remembering the many gems of wisdom and ways of knowing inherited from those who've come before you is helpful. Recall their wise sayings and give thanks for their passing such gems on to you.	Practicing gratitude		

Leading Well (LW) Dimension	Chapter(s)	Insights from LW	LW Practice	Rhythm (Frequency for This Practice)	Notes
Mental/ Intellectual	1	Reimagining can be an ongoing practice as situations in your life change.	Completing a vision board		
	5	Worship helps you access the living water.	Listening to your worship playlist		
Emotional	7	What you believe about yourself affects your emotional wellbeing. Limiting beliefs engender fear, doubt, and worry. Liberating beliefs release confidence, peace, and joy.	Exchanging limiting beliefs for liberating beliefs Identifying and internalizing scriptural truths that reinforce a liberating mindset		
Vocational	8	Leadership is a calling from God to fulfill one's life work.	Developing, reviewing, and/or refining your leadership purpose statement		

Leading Well (LW) Dimension	Chapter(s)	Insights from LW	LW Practice	Rhythm (Frequency for This Practice)	Notes
Physical	9	Engaging your spirit, soul, and body is a powerful form of prayer that can help you relieve stress, clear your mind, and talk to God.	Prayer walking		
			Getting regular exercise		
			Developing healthy eating practices that enhance mood and eliminating processed foods that tend to diminish the light within		
			Slowing down and getting adequate rest		

Leading Well (LW) Dimension	Chapter(s)	Insights from LW	LW Practice	Rhythm (Frequency for This Practice)	Notes
Environmental	9	In the physical sense, especially in winter, light can help enhance your mood. In the spiritual sense, light speaks of a leadership environment you want to help cultivate so you and others can thrive.	Outdoor prayer walking Using light therapy in the winter Working with a leadership coach or counselor and journaling to identify your leadership shadows		

ACKNOWLEDGMENTS

So much of leading well is practicing the spiritual discipline of gratitude. God brought this book together, from a word in my heart to a book in print.

I am grateful for the Holy Spirit's revelation, inspiration, communication, and manifestation of this book.

I am grateful that my life intersected with my two friends, Charley and Chandra, whose lives and deaths catapulted me on this journey to leading well.

I am grateful to the women of Christ Community Church who sojourned with me for a year as we studied the woman at the well, intending to become well-women. *Leading Well* was also inspired by this teaching series.

I am grateful for Brian Allain, leader of Publishing in Color, the platform that provides resources for writers of color and through which I found Lisa Crayton. Lisa collaborated with me to develop a bang-up proposal. Every coach needs a coach, and Lisa coached me through the proposal process and gave me the confidence to write this book my way. Thank you, Lisa, for your collaboration on making final edits with me after my mom passed. You are a godsend.

I am grateful for Jevon Bolden, the literary agent who saw the potential of this book and encouraged me to pray, hear from the Lord, and write what God had given to the audience God had directed. Jevon, it's truly a pleasure working with you, and I am grateful to be a part of the Embolden family of writers.

I am grateful to the Baker Books team. Thank you, Patnacia Goodman and the wonderful team of editors. I so appreciate your editorial guidance and support. I also appreciate the empathy and grace you extended to me during the difficult time finishing this book. Thank you, Sadina Grody Brott and your team for your insightful editing. Thank you, Olivia Peitsch and the entire marketing team, for your creative advice on marketing and Carson Kunnen for your guidance on positioning this book.

I am grateful for my sister friends who pray, read, unpack, listen, and pray some more: Debbye, Yolanda, Val, Wanda, Carmin, and Brenda. Thank you for being my sister friends!

I am grateful for my prayer team of cousins: Patti, Adell, and Larraine. We pray together weekly, and you've helped me to bathe this book in prayer.

I am grateful for my family, who supported me in writing this book. To my siblings and their families, thank you for all your encouragement. Carl, my loving husband, thank you for your support and encouragement and for every sacrifice you make that enables me to follow this passion.

And as I dedicated this book at the beginning, I am grateful for the caregiving time with my dear, sweet mother who encouraged me to keep on writing and loved me so well.

NOTES

Introduction

1. I spell *wholistic* in this way to point toward the goal of wholeness, which is the aim of *Leading Well*.

2. Jennifer A. Kingson, "Even Your Boss Wants to Quit," Axios, June 22, 2022, https://www.axios.com/2022/06/22/ceo-csuite-burnout-pandemic-great-resignation.

3. Kingson, *Even Your Boss Wants to Quit*.

4. "What Is Wellness?," Global Wellness Institute, accessed December 1, 2022, https://globalwellnessinstitute.org/what-is-wellness/.

5. Chanequa Walker-Barnes, *Too Heavy a Yoke: Black Women and the Burden of Strength* (Eugene, OR: Cascade Books, 2014).

6. Mercy Amba Oduyoye, "The Value of African Religious Beliefs and Practices for Christian Theology," in *African Theology en Route*, edited by Kofi Appiah-Kubi and Sergio Torres (Maryknoll, NY: Orbis Books, 1979), 111.

Chapter 1 Reimagine Your Leadership

1. Parker Palmer, *Let Your Life Speak: Listening to the Voice of Vocation* (San Francisco: Jossey-Bass, 1999).

2. Brené Brown, *Atlas of the Heart: Mapping Meaningful Connection and the Language of Human Connection* (New York: Random House, 2021), 18.

3. Bronwen Speedie, "Samaritan Sinner, Celebrated Saint: The Story of the First Christian Missionary," *CBE International Mutuality* (blog), December 4, 2016, https://www.cbeinternational.org/resource/article/mutuality-blog-magazine/samaritan-sinner-celebrated-saint-story-first-christian.

Chapter 2 Affirm Your Identity

1. Sylvia Ann Hewlett and Tai Green, *Black Women: Ready to Lead* (New York: Center for Talent Innovation, 2015), vii.

2. Center for Talent Innovation, "Being Black in Corporate America: An Intersectional Exploration," World Federation of Advertisers, December 9, 2019, https:// wfanet.org/knowledge/item/2019/12/09/Being-Black-in-Corporate-America -An-Intersectional-Exploration.

3. Elizabeth Hopper, "What Is a Microaggression? Everyday Insults with Harmful Effects," ThoughtCo, November 1, 2018, https://www.thoughtco.com /microaggression-definition-examples-4171853.

4. Derald Wing Sue, *Microaggressions in Everyday Life* (New York: Wiley, 2020).

5. "The Official Campaign of The CROWN Act," The CROWN Coalition, accessed August 7, 2022, https://www.thecrownact.com.

6. Mary-Frances Winters, *Black Fatigue: How Racism Erodes the Mind, Body, and Spirit* (Oakland: Berrett-Koehler, 2020), 121.

7. I define "working age" here as ages fifteen to seventy-four.

8. Centers for Disease Control and Prevention, "About Underlying Cause of Death, 1999–2020," CDC WONDER Online Database, accessed September 7, 2022, http://wonder.cdc.gov/ucd-icd10.html.

9. Arline T. Geronimus et al., "Do US Black Women Experience Stress-Related Accelerated Biological Aging?," *Human Nature* 21 (2010): 19–38, https://doi.org /10.1007/s12110-010-9078-0.

10. Gianna Melillo, "Racial Disparities Persist in Maternal Morbidity, Mortality and Infant Health," AJMC, June 13, 2020, https://www.ajmc.com/view/racial -disparities-persist-in-maternal-morbidity-mortality-and-infant-health.

11. Lottie L. Joiner, "Black May Not Crack, but We're Aging Faster Inside," *The Root*, November 20, 2013, https://www.theroot.com/black-may-not-crack -but-we-re-aging-faster-inside-1790898981.

12. Joiner, "Black May Not Crack."

13. BWHI Staff, "Black Women's Health Imperative Releases National Health Policy Agenda," Black Women's Health Imperative, October 27, 2020, https:// bwhi.org/2020/10/27/black-womens-health-imperative-releases-national-health -policy-agenda.

14. Alyssa Roat, "The Samaritans: Hope from the History of a Hated People," Bible Study Tools, February 5, 2020, https://www.biblestudytools.com/bible-study /topical-studies/the-samaritans-hope-from-the-history-of-a-hated-people.html.

15. I borrow the notions of drawing strength and stress from our cultures from a racial justice webinar hosted by Beth Zemsky, MAEd, LICSW, on the Intercultural Development Inventory (IDI) platform, https://idiinventory.com/.

Chapter 3 Ask for What You Need

1. Ruth Haley Barton, *Strengthening the Soul of Your Leadership: Seeking God in the Crucible of Ministry*, exp. ed. (Downers Grove, IL: InterVarsity Press, 2018), 25.

2. Barton, *Strengthening the Soul*, 25.

3. Peter Scazzero, *Emotionally Healthy Leadership: How Transforming Your Inner Life Will Deeply Transform Your Church, Team, and the World* (Grand Rapids: Zondervan, 2015), 25.

4. Scazzero, *Emotionally Healthy Leadership*, 50.

5. Scazzero, *Emotionally Healthy Leadership*, 25.

6. Scazzero, *Emotionally Healthy Leadership*, 25.

7. Scazzero, *Emotionally Healthy Leadership*, 25.

8. Walker-Barnes, *Too Heavy a Yoke*, 3.

9. Walker-Barnes, *Too Heavy a Yoke*, 3–4.

10. Walker-Barnes, *Too Heavy a Yoke*, 3.

11. Nancy S. Wiens, "Breath Prayer: An Ancient Spiritual Practice Connected with Science," Biologos, July 1, 2019, https://biologos.org/articles/breath-prayer-an-ancient-spiritual-practice-connected-with-science.

12. "Strong's H7307: *rûah*," Blue Letter Bible, accessed December 2, 2022, https://www.blueletterbible.org/lexicon/h7307/kjv/wlc/0-1/.

13. "Strong's G4151: *pneuma*," Blue Letter Bible, accessed December 2, 2022, https://www.blueletterbible.org/lexicon/g4151/kjv/tr/0-1/.

Chapter 4 Defy the Bias

1. Sandra M. Schneiders, *Written That You May Believe: Encountering Jesus in the Fourth Gospel*, rev. and exp. ed. (New York: Herder & Herder, 2003), 140.

2. Meredith J. C. Warren, "Five Husbands: Slut-Shaming the Samaritan Woman," *The Bible and Critical Theory* 17, no. 2 (2021): 51–69.

3. Warren, "Five Husbands," 60.

4. Online Etymology Dictionary, s.v. "patriarchy," accessed December 2, 2022, https://www.etymonline.com/word/patriarchy.

5. Schneiders, *Written That You May Believe*, 127.

6. Calum M. Carmichael, "Marriage and the Samaritan Woman," *New Testament Studies* 26, no. 3 (1980): 335.

7. Gerald Borchert, *John 1–11: An Exegetical and Theological Exposition of Holy Scripture*, vol. 25, The New American Commentary series, edited by E. Ray Clendenen and David S. Dockery (Nashville: Holman Reference, 1996), 205–6.

8. Kenneth O. Gangel, "John," *Holman New Testament Commentary* (Nashville: Holman Reference, 2000).

9. H. R. Reynolds, *John*, vol. 17, The Pulpit Commentary series, edited by Henry D. M. Spence-Jones (Peabody, MA: Hendrickson, 1985), https://ref.ly/o/tpc39/1619299?length=88.

10. John Triquilio and Kenneth Brighenti, *Women in the Bible for Dummies* (Hoboken, NJ: Wiley, 2011), 187.

11. James F. McGrath, "Ask a Scholar: Woman at the Well," Bible Odyssey, accessed December 2, 2022, https://www.bibleodyssey.org:443/tools/ask-a-scholar/woman-at-the-well.

12. Lynn H. Cohick, "Was the Samaritan Woman Really an Adulteress?," *Re-Word* (blog), October 12, 2015, https://www.christianitytoday.com/ct/2015/october/was-samaritan-woman-really-adulteress.html.

13. Cohick, "Was the Samaritan Woman Really an Adulteress?"

14. Cohick, "Was the Samaritan Woman Really an Adulteress?"

15. Rainesha L. Miller, "The Right to Be Angry: Black Women's Stress Appraisals, Anger Experiences and Expressions in the Context of Gendered Racism" (PhD diss., Oklahoma State University, August 2020), 2.

16. Carol Kuruvilla, "Southern Baptist Pastors Compare Kamala Harris to Bible's Queen Jezebel," *Huffpost*, February 9, 2021, https://www.huffpost.com /entry/kamala-harris-jezebel-pastors_n_601d967fc5b68e068fbe2c22.

17. "Black Women Disproportionately Experience Workplace Sexual Harassment, New NWLC Report Reveals," National Women's Law Center, August 2, 2018, https://nwlc.org/press-release/black-women-disproportionately-experience -workplace-sexual-harassment-new-nwlc-report-reveals/.

18. Daphna Motor, Jonathan B. Evans, Aleksander P. J. Ellis, and Lehman Benson III, "The Angry Black Woman Stereotype at Work," *Harvard Business Review*, January 31, 2022, https://hbr.org/2022/01/the-angry-black-woman-stereo type-at-work.

19. Walker-Barnes, *Too Heavy a Yoke*, 3.

Chapter 5 Perceive Your Possibilities

1. Frances Taylor Gench, *Back to the Well: Women's Encounters with Jesus in the Gospels* (Louisville: Westminster John Knox, 2004), 117.

2. Gench, *Back to the Well*, 117.

3. Schneiders, *Written That You May Believe*, 138.

4. Dorothy Lee, *Flesh and Glory: Symbolism, Gender and Theology in the Gospel of John* (New York: Crossroads, 2002), 76.

5. Lee, *Flesh and Glory*, 76.

6. Gench, *Back to the Well*, 117.

7. Gench, *Back to the Well*, 117.

8. Jeanne Porter King, *Influence Starts with "I": A Woman's Guide for Unleashing the Power of Leading from Within and Effecting Change around You* (Eugene, OR: Resource Publications, 2019), 7.

9. Feminist scholar Pauline Graham edited a book on Mary Parker Follett's writings titled *Mary Parker Follett: Prophet of Management* (Washington, DC: Beard Books, 2003).

10. Pauline Graham, ed., *Mary Parker Follett Prophet of Management: A Celebration of the Writings from the 1920s* (Washington, DC: Beard Books, 2003), 23, 103.

11. Melva Wilson Costen, *African American Christian Worship*, 2nd ed. (Nashville: Abingdon Press, 2007), 5.

12. Lisa Allen, *A Womanist Theology of Worship: Liturgy, Justice, and Communal Righteousness* (Maryknoll, NY: Orbis Books, 2021), 59.

13. Allen, *Womanist Theology*, 56.

14. Gench, *Back to the Well*, 117.

15. Austa Somvichian-Clausen, "How Stacey Abrams Helped Get Out the Black Vote in Georgia," *Changing America*, November 10, 2020, https://thehill .com/changing-america/respect/diversity-inclusion/525387-how-stacey-abrams -helped-get-out-the-black-vote/.

16. Constance Grady, "Kamala Harris: 'I May Be the First Woman to Hold This Office. But I Won't Be the Last,'" *Vox*, November 7, 2020, https://www.vox .com/policy-and-politics/21554699/kamala-harris-victory-acceptance-speech.

17. Grady, "Kamala Harris."

Chapter 6 Trust Our Ways of Knowing

1. Patricia Hill Collins, *Black Feminist Thought: Knowledge, Consciousness, and the Politics of Empowerment* (New York: Routledge, 1991), 256.

2. Collins, *Black Feminist Thought*, 257.

3. "Strong's G1492: *eidō*," Blue Letter Bible, accessed December 2, 2022, https://www.blueletterbible.org/lexicon/g1492/nlt/mgnt/0-1/.

4. Schneiders, *Written That You May Believe*, 138.

5. Schneiders, *Written That You May Believe*, 138.

6. Collins, *Black Feminist Thought*, 257.

7. bell hooks, *Talking Back: Thinking Feminist, Thinking Black* (Boston: South End Press, 1989), 131.

8. Collins, *Black Feminist Thought*, 262.

9. Collins, *Black Feminist Thought*, 264.

10. Collins, *Black Feminist Thought*, 265.

11. Collins, *Black Feminist Thought*, 266.

12. Gench, *Back to the Well*, 117.

13. Schneiders, *Written That You May Believe*, 139.

14. Sojourner Truth, "Speech Entitled 'Ain't I a Woman?' Delivered at the 1851 Women's Convention in Akron, Ohio," Andrew Jackson's Hermitage, accessed December 8, 2022, https://thehermitage.com/wp-content/uploads/2016/02/Sojourner-Truth_Aint-I-a-Woman_1851.pdf.

15. "WATCH: Jackson Tears Up, as Sen. Booker Says She's Earned Her Historic Supreme Court Nomination," (13:46) YouTube video, 19:53, uploaded by PBS News Hour, March 23, 2022, https://www.youtube.com/watch?v=VjjvNLMyNS4.

16. "WATCH: Jackson Tears Up," (14:22).

Chapter 7 Leave Your Old Water Jars Behind

1. Collins, *Black Feminist Thought*, 69.

2. The Quaker Oats Company, "Aunt Jemima Brand to Remove Image from Packaging and Change Brand Name," *PR Newswire*, June 17, 2020, https://www.prnewswire.com/news-releases/aunt-jemima-brand-to-remove-image-from-packaging-and-change-brand-name-301078593.html.

3. Lynne St. Clair Darden, "A Womanist-Postcolonial Reading of the Samaritan Woman at the Well and Mary Magdalene at the Tomb," in *I Found God in Me: A Womanist Biblical Hermeneutic Reader*, edited by Mitzi J. Smith (Eugene, OR: Cascade Books), 195.

4. Schneiders, *Written That You May Believe*, 141.

5. King, *Influence Starts with "I,"* 44.

6. Dave Paunesku, "5 Strategies for Changing Mindsets," *Learning Mindset* (blog), March 30, 2019, https://medium.com/learning-mindset/5-strategies-for-changing-mindsets-ce2de5f92056.

7. Elizabeth Scott, "What Is a Toxic Relationship?," Very Well Mind, August 26, 2022, https://www.verywellmind.com/toxic-relationships-4174665.

8. Scott, "What Is a Toxic Relationship?"

9. Scott, "What Is a Toxic Relationship?"

Chapter 8 Follow the Call

1. Merriam-Webster, s.v. "life's work," accessed November 30, 2022, https://www.merriam-webster.com/dictionary/life%27s%20work.

2. Palmer, *Let Your Life Speak*, 4.

3. Palmer, *Let Your Life Speak*, 2.

4. Palmer, *Let Your Life Speak*, 2.

5. Palmer, *Let Your Life Speak*, 3.

6. Palmer, *Let Your Life Speak*, 4–5.

7. As quoted in Lay Kim, "Life Can Only Be Understood Backwards Meaning Explained," *Quotationize* (blog), July 25, 2021, https://quotationize.com/life-can-only-be-understood-backwards-meaning-explained/.

8. Nicholas Pearce, *The Purpose Path: A Guide to Pursuing Your Authentic Life's Work* (New York: St. Martin's Essential, 2019), xv.

9. Frederick Buechner, *Wishful Thinking: A Seeker's ABC* (San Francisco: HarperSanFrancisco, 1993), 119.

10. Adapted from King, *Influence Starts with "I,"* 21.

Chapter 9 Lead On with Light

1. "Word Wealth," in *New Spirit-Filled Life Bible* (Nashville: Thomas Nelson, 2002), 1467. John 12:46.

2. St. Clair Darden, *A Womanist-Postcolonial Reading*, 221.

3. Jeanne L. Porter, "Lead on with Light: A Phenomenology of Leadership As Seen in Gloria Naylor's *Mama Day*," in *Nature of a Sistuh: Black Women's Lived Experiences in Contemporary Culture*, edited by Trevy McDonald and T. Ford-Ahmed (Durham, NC: Carolina Academic Press, 1999), 266–78.

4. Alisha Rahaman Sarkur, "Ring Cam Footage in Texas Shows Young White Boy Cracking Whip against Black Family's Front Door," *Independent*, May 30, 2022, https://www.independent.co.uk/news/world/americas/crime/texas-boy-whip-black-family-video-b2080855.html.

5. "Mass Shooting in Buffalo," *New York Times*, May 15, 2022, https://www.nytimes.com/2022/05/15/briefing/mass-shooting-buffalo-new-york.html.

6. Gloria Naylor, *Mama Day* (New York: Vintage, 1989), 110.

7. Naylor, *Mama Day*, 110.

8. Naylor, *Mama Day*, 110.

9. Naylor, *Mama Day*, 110.

10. "Seasonal Affective Disorder," Mayo Clinic, accessed September 28, 2022, https://www.mayoclinic.org/diseases-conditions/seasonal-affective-disorder/symptoms-causes/syc-20364651.

11. Norman E. Rosenthal, *Winter Blues: Everything You Need to Know to Beat Seasonal Affective Disorder*, fourth ed. (New York: Guilford Press, 2012).

12. Palmer, *Let Your Life Speak*, 78.

13. Ruchika Tulshyan and Jodi-Ann Burey, "Stop Telling Women They Have Imposter Syndrome," *Harvard Business Review*, February 11, 2021, https://hbr.org/2021/02/stop-telling-women-they-have-imposter-syndrome.

14. Tulshyan and Burey, "Stop Telling Women."

15. Tulshyan and Burey, "Stop Telling Women."

16. Tulshyan and Burey, "Stop Telling Women."

17. Dr. Ijeoma Opara (@IjeomaOparaPHD), "No amount of DEI trainings can protect Black people in America," Twitter post, May 15, 2022, https://twitter.com/IjeomaOparaPHD/status/1525939515357028353.

18. Special thanks to Rev. Dr. Jeremiah Wright for sharing the ethnomusicology of "Siyahamba" and other cultural gems.

Chapter 10 Lead with Legacy in Mind

1. Online Etymology Dictionary, s.v. "legacy," accessed December 2, 2022, https://www.etymonline.com/search?q=legacy.

2. Online Etymology Dictionary, s.v. "legacy."

3. Vocabulary.com, s.v. "legacy," accessed December 2, 2022, https://www.vocabulary.com/dictionary/legacy.

4. Susan Bosak, "What Is Legacy?," Legacy Project, accessed December 2, 2022, https://www.legacyproject.org/guides/whatislegacy.html.

5. Speedie, "Samaritan Sinner, Celebrated Saint."

6. "St. Photini, the Samaritan Woman," Antiochian Orthodox Christian Archdiocese of North America, accessed October 9, 2022, http://ww1.antiochian.org/st-photini-samaritan-woman.

7. Speedie, "Samaritan Sinner, Celebrated Saint."

8. Eva Catafygiotu Topping, *Holy Mothers of Orthodoxy: Women and the Church* (Minneapolis: Light & Life, 1987), 57.

9. Topping, *Holy Mothers of Orthodoxy*, 57.

10. Speedie, "Samaritan Sinner, Celebrated Saint."

11. Speedie, "Samaritan Sinner, Celebrated Saint."

12. Speedie, "Samaritan Sinner, Celebrated Saint."

13. Topping, *Holy Mothers of Orthodoxy*, 57.

14. Topping, *Holy Mothers of Orthodoxy*, 57.

15. Topping, *Holy Mothers of Orthodoxy*, 57.

16. "CSU Pratt Center: Fostering Success, Leadership and Hope," Cleveland State University, December 7, 2021, https://www.csuohio.edu/news/csu-pratt-center-fostering-success-leadership-and-hope.

17. Jarrett Pratt, personal interview, May 27, 2022.

18. "'The Beloved Community' is a term that was first coined in the early days of the twentieth Century by the philosopher-theologian Josiah Royce, who founded the Fellowship of Reconciliation; The King Center, accessed February, 2023, https://thekingcenter.org/about-tkc/the-king-philosophy/.

19. Jeanne Theoharis, "'I Am Not a Symbol, I Am an Activist': The Untold Story of Coretta Scott King," *Guardian*, February 3, 2018, https://www.theguardian.com/world/2018/feb/03/coretta-scott-king-extract.

20. Barbara Ransby, "Coretta Scott King Was More Than Civil Rights Widow," *Progressive Magazine*, February 1, 2006, https://progressive.org/op-eds/coretta-scott-king-civil-rights-widow/.

21. Ransby, "Coretta Scott King Was More."

22. Brandeis "Nilaja" Green, "Strong Like My Mama: The Legacy of 'Strength,' Depression, and Suicidality in African American Women," *Women & Therapy* 42, nos. 3–4 (2019): 265–88, https://doi.org/10.1080/02703149.2019.1622909.

Closing

1. Maya Angelou (@DrMayaAngelou), "Each of us has that right, that possibility, to invent ourselves daily," Twitter post, March 1, 2019, https://twitter.com /drmayaangelou/status/1101546857908633601?lang=en.

Jeanne Porter King, PhD, is an author, consultant, pastor, and leadership coach specializing in women's leadership. A trusted teacher and guide who has taught leadership at both the undergrad and seminary levels, Dr. Porter King is the founder and president of TransPorter Group Inc., a consulting company focused on leadership development. She is passionate about developing existing and emerging women leaders. Her goal is to encourage and empower more Black women to lead well. She lives in South Holland, Illinois, with her husband, Pastor Carl E. King.